Dedicated to American Liberty in all its messiness.

Author's Note

Some of the profiles in this book bear the names of living persons. In each of them, I have relied only on public information, intending to lay out fact-based narratives that avoid overt judgments. (I'll leave that to the readers, if there are any.) Some profiles have been altered in the interest of privacy. Some historical figures are composites, based on documented events. Any visual likeness to any person, living or dead, is pure, dumb luck.

Special Thanks to:

James David Audlin
Joshua Barron
Samuel Brown
Myles Hall
Nathan B. King
Jennifer Taylor
Lydia Temonia
Venita Upton

John G. Cunyus
Author
www.JohnCunyus.com

THE LIBERTY TREE: One Hundred Faces of America

An Illustrated History

ISBN: 978-1-936497-478-7

Searchlight Press
Who are you looking for?
Publishers of thoughtful Christian books
5634 Ledgestone Drive
Dallas, Texas. USA
75214-2026
www.JohnCunyus.com

TABLE OF CONTENTS

The Liberty Tree

The original Liberty Tree was an enormous elm which stood near Boston Common. It was planted in 1646 by the original wave of English settlers in what was then the Massachusetts Bay Colony. The tree grew with the settlement.

Its association with Liberty began in 1765. The British Parliament, far away across the Atlantic, determined to claw back some of its huge expenses in the recently-completed French and Indian War. The war permanently ended French threats to Britain's American colonies, and guaranteed the colonists a greater measure of security against Indian raids as well.

It seemed only natural in distant London that those who benefited from the war should help pay its expenses. Parliament imposed the Stamp Tax on colonial commerce to do just that. The colonists, however, weren't consulted.

One principle in English law was that English citizens could not be taxed unless their representatives approved. The colonists at that time considered themselves English, possessing all the rights English people in the native land did. Yet they had no representation in the British Parliament. The cry of "No taxation without representation" boiled up as colonial fury against the Stamp Act ignited.

In 1765, a group called "The Sons of Liberty" rallied around the huge elm tree near Boston Common for the first time. It soon became a symbol of resistance. In 1775, open warfare began between the American colonists and their British overlords. British forces initially held Boston, before George Washington's Continental Army outflanked them on Dorchester Heights and forced them to withdraw.

Before their withdrawal was complete, British loyalists cut down the Liberty Tree, hoping to strike a blow against the movement it had come to represent. Thus, the original Liberty Tree passed into history. The symbol, however, endured.

This book tells the partial stories of one hundred who have been part of the story of Liberty in North America. Many of those pictured did NOT experience Liberty. Some actively sought to take Liberty away from others. The tree in this picture reflects that, all signs of living boughs and leaves absent. It may be that this Liberty Tree, like the original in Boston, is dead.

But many of those pictured here DID attain Liberty. Some of them managed to survive terrible hardships in doing so. Others endured wars and terrible violence on behalf of (or at times against) the cause of Liberty. Some are heroes. Some are survivors. Some, likely, are villains.

But Liberty's story isn't over. Perhaps the Liberty Tree pictured here is dead and the ideal was an illusion. Perhaps the villains won.

Then again, elm trees are not evergreens. They lose their leaves in Autumn, remain bare and empty in Winter, then spring to life again in Spring. Despite an imported disease that killed three in four of North America's elms in the 20th Century, the species survives.

Perhaps this Liberty Tree is one of the survivors. Perhaps it merely waits for springtime and the struggles have not been in vain. Perhaps the ideal of Liberty lives on.

In many ways, that is up to us.

Kitty Unami

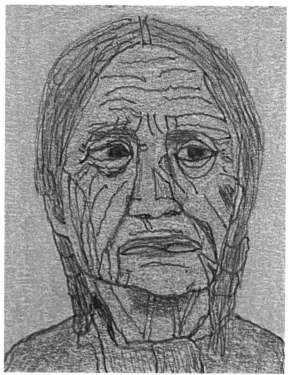

Kittaptoni "Kitty" Unami was a Lenape (Delaware) woman whose exact dates of birth and death are lost to history. She lived during the 17th Century, near the northeast coast of North America on the Atlantic Ocean.

The Lenape people's first contact with English settlers took place along what is now the Delaware River, in the Eastern US State of Delaware, in 1610.

The English couldn't pronounce "Lenape" (It's "luh-NAY-pay") There are various versions of how the Lenape came to be called Delaware.

As a prologue to the story of Liberty, today's Delaware nations are based in Oklahoma, half a continent away from their East Coast homelands –

survivors of multiple forced relocations.

Lots of folks moved West.

Some did it by their own free choice, seeking Liberty.

Some did it to build better lives for themselves and their children.

Some did it by accident.

Some did it fleeing a life left behind.

Some did it at the point of a gun.

However it happened, they went.

However it happened, here we are.

Conrad Heyer

Conrad Heyer lived during the Revolutionary War period in the British colony of Delaware, not far from where Kitty Unami's ancestors first encountered English settlers. His ancestors, however, came from Germany rather than England. Most of the early German settlers came to the colonies to escape religious violence in their homeland.

When the Revolutionary War broke out, Captain Jonathan Caldwell recruited Conrad and many others like him into the First Delaware Regiment of the Continental Army. They were crack troops, and they played a crucial role in the army's narrow escape from the British in New York. By the end of 1776, Washington had called on them many times, and they had risen to the occasion.

So it was that on Christmas night, 1776, Conrad and his Regiment crossed the Delaware River with Washington from Pennsylvania into New Jersey. They fell upon the unsuspecting Hessian garrison holding the town of Trenton for the British, scoring a dramatic American victory at a moment when patriot morale was at a low point.

The Hessians themselves were Germans, hired as soldiers by the British king to help fight his war against the colonists. When the war ended, most of their survivors returned to Germany. Quite a few of them, though, chose to stay after the war in the new nation they had fought to oppose.

Heyer survived the war and returned home to Delaware, yet there was an irony in his returning. Having fought a war ostensibly for Liberty, he lived in a jurisdiction that denied Liberty to many of its residents. Delaware not only permitted the practice of slavery, it made the condition hereditary. If an enslaved person gave birth to a child in Delaware or any other slaveholding State, the child, too, was enslaved.

The State of Delaware was south of the Mason-Dixon line, which divided the early United States between slaveholding and non-slaveholding regions. North of the line, New York began the process of formal abolition as early as 1799. Many of the other "free" States followed suit, though slavery remained legal in some until final Abolition in 1865.

Most of the States south of the line joined the Confederacy during the Secession Crisis of 1861 after Abraham Lincoln's first election as President. They feared the Anti-Slavery platform of that era's Republican Party and the future of their economic model. Delaware remained in the Union. A Civil War between the northern and southern States raged from 1861-1865.

The Union Army liberated enslaved persons in the territories it reconquered from the States in rebellion beginning in 1863, following Lincoln's

Emancipation Proclamation. Slaveholding in Delaware did not end until the 13th Amendment to the U. S. Constitution came into effect in 1865, after the war ended.

Conrad Heyer spent his long life enjoying his personal Liberty, no doubt aware of those denied it among his neighbors. The contradiction between Liberty and slavery cut to the heart of the American story from its earliest days.

Simon Dansk

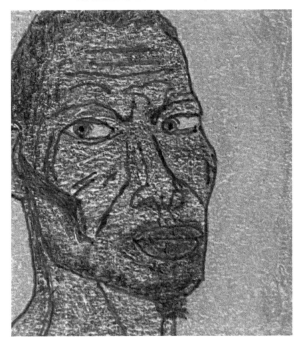

This is Simon Dansk. At least that is what his captors called him. He did not come to this Liberty party by choice.

As a youth, he was betrayed by a neighboring clan, kidnapped, and sold into slavery. He survived the infamous Middle Passage and was brought in chains to the island of St. Jan in the Danish West Indies. He had been trafficked as part of the lethal "triangular trade," which brought sugar from the Caribbean to Europe, firearms and other manufactured goods from Europe to Africa, and human captives from Africa to the Caribbean.

Simon was held in forced labor under grueling conditions on a sugar cane plantation for the rest of his life. His homeland, his tribe, his family, and even his given name disappeared under the grip of slavery. The bankruptcy of the Danish West Indies Company in 1754 merely led to the islands being taken over directly by the Danish crown.

He died in 1790, having lost touch with all parts of his past except for his longing for Liberty.

Denmark abolished slavery in the islands in 1848, and sold the islands to the United States in 1917. Many of Simon's descendants remain there to this day.

Nancy Daniels

Nancy Daniels, so named by her captors, was born among the Igbo people in West Africa around 1751. Kidnapped as a young teenager, she was trafficked into slavery and also survived the infamous "Middle Passage" across the Atlantic. She never saw her family, people, or homeland again.

As a young woman just entering prime childbearing years, she was an especially valuable "commodity" when sold to a family of English settlers in Barbados. She survived wars, revolutions, and hurricanes, living long enough to be emancipated when the British Empire abolished slavery in 1834. At that point, though, she had no means of returning home.

Her photo was taken in 1855, making her one of the first women of color captured on film. She died shortly after, her Igbo name lost to history.

Shapley Ross

Captain Shapley Prince Ross, 1811-1889, was a pioneer settler of Texas. Born in Kentucky, he moved with his family first to Missouri, where he was married. Ross emigrated to what was then the Republic of Texas in 1839.

In those tumultuous years, Ross settled his family first in Milam County, northeast of Austin. After serving on the committee to choose the Milam County seat, he moved briefly to Austin. Given the violent nature of life on the frontier, Ross joined the Texas Rangers, a State-sponsored militia for collective defense. He rose to the rank of Captain, serving under Jack Hayes.

Elected a Ranger captain by his fellow Rangers, he was assigned to defend settlements near the Brazos River, a hundred miles northeast of Austin. Ross built the first house in what became Waco. As the town grew up around him, he built the first hotel there as well. His duties expanded over the years to include being postmaster, Indian agent, and cattle drover.

Despite the isolation of the frontier, Ross was determined that his children receive an education. His son, Lawrence Sullivan "Sul" Ross, graduated from Baylor University, which was chartered in 1845 by the last Congress of the Republic of Texas prior to annexation by the United States. The younger Ross went on to live a storied life in the emergence of post Civil War Texas.

Shapley Ross owned slaves in Missouri prior to his relocation to Texas, according to US Census Data. He does not seem to have continued the practice after his move to Texas, according to the last pre-Civil War US Census. Though Sul Ross, Shapley's son, rose to prominence in the Confederate Army, the younger Ross showed a marked interest in the welfare and education of Black Texans during his service both as Governor of the State and as President of the Agricultural and Mechanical College of Texas (today's Texas A&M University).

However fitfully, however hindered by the assumptions and prejudices of the times, Shapley Ross seems to have watered the Liberty Tree during his long life in Texas.

John "Jack" Merrifield

Jack Merrifield was born in 1792 in Kentucky. A veteran of the War of 1812, he served under Andrew Jackson in the Battle of New Orleans. After the war, Merrifield returned to Kentucky and started a family.

A cholera epidemic killed his wife and daughter in Kentucky, leading Jack to send his sons to Texas to scout a place to resettle. The Merrifields arrived around 1847, and Jack's first property deed in Texas was filed in 1851. Jack built an additional room onto the two-room log cabin already on the property to house his second wife and eleven surviving children.

Merrifield spent the rest of his life there, a couple of miles west of the Trinity River in the heart of what became the city of Oak Cliff. In 1903, Oak Cliff was annexed into Dallas, across the river on the east bank of the Trinity.

Sometimes, Liberty looks like a three-room cabin housing thirteen souls on the edge of the frontier.

Deacon Samuel Sharpe

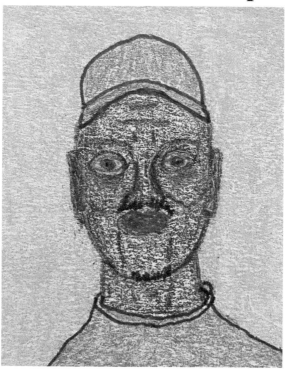

Samuel Sharpe was born into slavery on the British-ruled island of Jamaica in 1801. The British Empire had long profited from the sugar produced under the plantation system maintained there. By the time of Sharpe's birth, however, British public opinion was turning against slavery.

Sharpe came into contact with Baptist missionaries from England as a youth. He was baptized and allowed by his 'owner' to learn to read and write. In short order, Sharpe mastered these skills and became an avid reader and teacher of Bible in the Jamaican Baptist Churches.

Sharpe, convinced by the New Testament that slavery was un-Christian, shared that message in the churches with other enslaved persons. He closely followed the debates reported in Jamaican newspapers as Britain's distant

Parliament discussed slavery.

At Christmas 1832, Sharpe organized a work stoppage in response to those enslaved being denied the customary full holiday break. Because of his influence, many other enslaved Baptists decided to join the protest. On Christmas Day, the protest escalated. While Sharpe and those with him only envisioned a work stoppage, many others rebelled violently against their condition.

The local militia quickly put down the rebellion by force. Sharpe, as the leader, was arrested, tried, convicted, and hanged, despite pleas on his behalf by both white and Black Baptist leaders. He reportedly said on his way to execution, "I would rather hang on those gallows than live as a slave."

Shaken by the violence in Jamaica, Britain's Parliament banned slavery empire-wide in 1834.

Deacon Samuel Sharpe watered the Liberty Tree with his own blood.

Will Turner

Will Turner was born into slavery in the 1830s in North Carolina. At age 16, he escaped into deep swampland, hunted by dogs and men alike. He endured six weeks of hardship before reaching a port of relative safety.

His whereabouts thereafter are unknown.

Will embodied New Hampshire's state motto:

"Live free or die."

John Watson

John Watson entered this story in 1808 in North Carolina. His father died when he was six. He and his mother moved to Tennessee in 1826.

John began his move to Texas in 1849 as a married man with many children. He built a houseboat to hold his family and possessions and used it to float down the Tennessee River to Arkansas. The Watsons put in a crop at Pine Bluff, Arkansas, that year, and arrived in East Texas in 1850. He fathered fourteen (14) children in all.

John opposed secession in Texas, according to his Pastor, J. H. Livsey. He believed a settlement could have been arbitrated without war, had it been handled wisely. He was not a slaveholder.

When old John heard news of Jefferson Davis's death, he said, "If I can't outdo him any other way, I can outlive him."

Jefferson Davis had been President of the Confederacy, which formed from the seceded States.

John Watson died in 1900. In his eulogy, Brother Livsey added, "In politics, Bro. Watson was a Republican, but there was something about the man that robbed the name 'Republican' of all its opprobrium."

Mary Thompson

Mary Thompson was born into slavery in the early 1850s. She was old enough by the time liberation came to remember her status and to hope for better things.

Thompson married a freedman and settled into the sharecropping experience in Alabama's "Black Belt." She gave birth to ten children and, with her husband, played a central part in the Colored Methodist Church that emerged from the existing Methodist congregation in her community, dominated as it was by former slaveholders.

She never learned to read or write, but worked hard to support the tiny community school and its one teacher. Some of her children did learn to read and write, then drifted away to towns and cities in areas less haunted by brutal memories.

Mary remained behind, living fifty years as a widow after her husband died. The blessings of Liberty she hoped for as a newly freed young woman never quite materialized to her satisfaction. Nevertheless, she saw three generations born in the small measure of freedom they had gained. To her dying day she never gave up hope for better things ahead.

Sojourner Truth

Sojourner Truth was born Isabella Bomfree in Ulster County, New York in 1797. Ulster County remained predominantly Dutch-speaking at the time of her birth.

Forced into a breeder's marriage, Bomfree birthed five children between 1815 and 1826, the year she escaped with her infant daughter.

In 1827, New York became the first U. S. State to abolish slavery. This culminated a twenty-eight-year process that began under Governor John Jay in 1799. Bomfree successfully sued under the new law for the return of her

5-year-old son, who had been sold to slaveholders in Alabama.

In 1830, she moved with her family to New York City to work for a Christian minister. Swept up in the religious revivals of the day, she became a traveling evangelist.

While traveling, she met William Lloyd Garrison and Frederick Douglass, leading abolitionists at the time. Both encouraged her to incorporate her own story of enslavement and escape into her speaking, which she did.

She legally changed her name to Sojourner Truth in 1843.

In 1851, she dictated her book, *The Narrative of Sojourner Truth*, to Olive Gilbert. Thereafter, she supported herself by public speaking and book sales. Truth herself never learned to read or write.

At 6'0" tall, she was an imposing figure on a speaker's platform, at a time when significant audiences attended public speeches. She gave one such speech to a women's rights conference in Akron, Ohio. The speech, *Ain't I a Woman?*, advocated not just for Liberty for Black women, but for suffrage, as well.

During the Civil War, she recruited young men into the Union Army, and organized supplies for Black troops at the front. After the War, she worked with customary energy with the Freedmen's Bureau.

Sojourner Truth continued her public advocacy until old age rendered it impossible. She died in 1883 in Battle Creek, Michigan.

She watered the Liberty Tree with her own blood, sweat, and tears.

Abraham Lincoln

Abraham Lincoln joined the dance of Liberty in 1809, born in a log cabin in a remote area of Kentucky. Valid titles to land were hard to come by in Kentucky in those days. Disputes over land ownership led Lincoln's parents to relocate twice during his childhood: first to another site in Kentucky and then to southern Indiana.

Like many on what was then the western frontier, young Lincoln had little opportunity for formal education. Despite that, he learned to read and write, and voraciously read whatever books he came across. His particular favorites included *The Bible*, *A Pilgrim's Progress*, *Aesop's Fables*, *Robinson Crusoe*, and Mason Weems' *The Life of Washington*. Young Lincoln spent so much time reading and scribbling notes that some of his neighbors mistook him for lazy.

In 1818, Lincoln's mother died. His father remarried, bringing his new wife and her three children to the Indiana farm. The second wife also died shortly thereafter, followed by Lincoln's older sister, who died during childbirth. In 1830, the Lincoln family relocated to southern Illinois. After helping get them established on the new land, he set out on his own at age 21.

He read for and passed the Bar in Illinois, becoming a lawyer. Lincoln's talents rapidly became evident. In 1837, he relocated to Springfield, Illinois, which had been chosen as the State's new capital. Lincoln married Mary Todd there in 1841.

As his legal career prospered, he became involved in politics as well, serving several terms in the Illinois Legislature and one in the U. S. House of Representatives. Lincoln was a member of the Whig Party when he entered public life. The Whigs opposed the expansion of slavery, an issue with which Lincoln vigorously agreed. When the Whig Party disintegrated in the 1840s and 1850s, Lincoln joined the Republican Party, founded in Ripon, Wisconsin, in 1854.

The Republicans were committed to "free labor" and determined to eventually abolish slavery, In the interim, they passionately opposed the expansion of slavery into new territories, and laws forcing residents of non-slave States to capture and return those who escaped enslavement.

After losing to Democrat Stephen Douglas in 1858 in a race for the U. S. Senate in Illinois, Lincoln was nominated for President by the Republicans in 1860. It was only the second presidential election the party had contested. He carried eighteen States and 60% of the electoral vote, though he only carried 40% of the popular vote in a particularly fractured political year. In many of the slave States, his name was not even on the ballot.

Before he was inaugurated, the country began breaking apart. Seven States initially seceded from the Union, forming the Confederacy on February 4, 1861. All cited the threat to slavery. An uneasy truce held until after the inauguration.

On the morning of April 12, 1861, just over a month after Lincoln's inauguration, southern forces opened fire on the Union garrison at Fort Sumter, South Carolina. Civil War erupted between the opposing sides. At this fraught moment, four more States seceded and joined the Confederacy.

Lincoln's initial determination was to preserve the Union. As the war dragged on, though, he saw the necessity of striking at the institution of slavery in order to break the economic power of the rebellion. After the Union victory at Antietam, Maryland, in 1862, he issued the Emancipation Proclamation freeing slaves in States that had rebelled.

As the tide of war turned decisively against the rebellion, Lincoln lobbied for and Congress passed the Thirteenth Amendment to the U. S. Constitution in January of 1865, abolishing slavery nationwide. Approved by the necessary number of State legislatures, excluding, of course those in rebellion, the amendment became the law of the land in December of 1865.

By then, the war had ended in a Union victory. Lincoln did not live to see the emancipation, having been murdered in Washington by a Southern sympathizer on April 15, 1865.

He remains to this date perhaps the most influential advocate for Liberty in the history of the Americas.

Marcel Fauvrot

Like so many who inherited their status as property merely by being born, Marcel Fauvrot never knew his birthdate. He came into the world in the mid-1830s on a plantation in southern Louisiana.

In the chaos of the first years of the Civil War, Fauvrot escaped his captors and joined Benjamin Butler's Union Army in New Orleans. He served for the rest of the war, seeing bitter action in the struggle to free his own kith and kin.

After the war, Fauvrot faced the recurring traumas that have afflicted military veterans before and since. Despite his service, society remained harshly segregated. When Reconstruction ended in the 1870s and the Union Army withdrew, the gains the Black community had made were almost entirely clawed back.

Fauvrot, despite having risked his own life in the cause of Liberty, sank into a spiral of alcohol and despair before his death in 1880. The U. S. government gave him one piece of recognition for his service: a burial plot and gravestone in the military cemetery at Chalmette, Louisiana.

Even there, Fauvrot and his fellow "colored troops," so designated on their tombstones, lie segregated from their white brothers-in-arms.

John Bell Hood

John Bell Hood was born into a well-connected family in Owingsville, Kentucky, in 1831. Those connections led to his appointment in 1849 to the U. S. Military Academy at West Point, New York. Hood was a below-average student, finishing 44th in a class of 52. He was also a hellraiser, only four demerits short of expulsion by the time he graduated in 1853.

After an Army posting in California, he was assigned to the Texas frontier in 1857 as part of the elite U. S. 2nd Cavalry. He took an arrow through the hand in action against the Comanche later that year.

After the bombardment of Fort Sumter, Hood resigned from the U. S. Army. Disgusted with his native Kentucky's neutrality, he declared himself a Texan and was commissioned into the Confederate States Army. He led what came to be known as known as Hood's Texas Brigade, an elite formation in Robert E Lee's Army of Northern Virginia. He gained his reputation as "the gallant Hood of Texas" serving under Lee.

At Gettysburg, Hood took a shell fragment to the left arm while leading a successful attack. This time, the wound was severe, and he permanently lost use of the arm. After recovering, he was sent under General James Longstreet's command to reinforce Confederate forces in the West. In September of 1863, Hood lost his right leg to a sniper's bullet at the Battle of Chickamauga.

He convalesced, and yet again returned to command under General Joseph Johnston. Johnston's army was trying to defend Georgia against General William T. Sherman's invasion. Hood led his corps so aggressively that, in mid-1864, Confederate President Jefferson Davis relieved Johnston and made Hood the overall commander.

While he had gained fame as a corps commander, he was in over his head commanding an army. Sherman's troops beat back his initial attacks and forced him to retreat from Atlanta. Hood swung west to threaten Sherman's supply lines, anticipating Sherman would follow him. Sherman didn't.

Hood then attempted an invasion of Tennessee to try and stem the Union tide. Though his army was technically the victor at the Battle of Franklin, his straight ahead, frontal assault left thousands of his soldiers dead on the battlefield.

Despite that, he led what remained of them on to the outskirts of Nashville, capital of the State and target of his invasion. All the while, whenever the army moved his aides had to strap him to his horse to keep up because of his disabilities. The Confederate forces suffered a catastrophic defeat at Nashville, outnumbered and overwhelmed by Union troops under General George Thomas.

Hood led the survivors back to Mississippi, voluntarily giving up command of the army. He was making his way back to Texas when the war ended.

After the war, Hood moved with his wife and eleven children to New Orleans, scratching out a living as a businessman. He, his wife, and his eldest daughter died of yellow fever within days of each other in 1879, leaving behind ten destitute orphans. His former soldiers stepped up collectively to raise the children.

Hood was regarded as a hero in the post-war South. Hindsight shows him to have been overly aggressive, heedless of the lives of his troops, and unwilling to consider tactical alternatives.

Passionate but misguided, John Bell Hood suffered greatly for his misconception of Liberty. He inflicted great suffering as well.

Tom Southwell

Fur traders and trappers began blazing the Oregon Trail as early as 1811 from what was then the American far west along the Mississippi River. The first wagon train moved west on the trail in 1836. Emigrant traffic increased through the years as the trail improved.

Pioneer settlers in the still-unincorporated region of Oregon prohibited slavery in the organic law they passed in 1843. The following year, the same body voted to exclude free Blacks as well. Though the Black exclusion law was repealed in 1845, the sentiment remained.

Oregon was incorporated as a Territory in 1848, after American victory in the Mexican War secured the U. S. position on the West Coast. Oregon's first Constitution in 1857 both forbade slavery and excluded free Blacks. The distant Congress in Washington admitted Oregon as a State on the basis of its new Constitution in 1858.

Tom Southwell, born in Missouri in the 1840s, traveled the Oregon Trail as a child with his family and enslavers. When they arrived in Oregon, they stayed away from the emerging population centers as a way of avoiding the prohibition of slavery.

When the Civil War broke out in distant South Carolina, the U. S. government withdrew its regular army units and sent them east. The State replaced them with its own, hastily reorganized militia, worried about unrest among Indian tribes in the absence of federal troops.

Against this backdrop, Southwell's 'owners' decided to return to east as well, so as not to lose their human 'property' in the chaos. Southwell, now a teenager, escaped from the caravan during a bandit attack somewhere in the vastness of western Nebraska.

He briefly joined the bandits, but they soon turned on him, plotting to sell him back to his purported 'owners.' Southwell fought his way out of the bandit entrapment, determined never to return to enslavement.

He succeeded, escaping southwestward and eventually settling in Colorado. He lived the rest of his life there, marrying and raising family as a free man in a free State. Southwell valued intensely the often-praised "blessings of Liberty," having known life's brutality without it.

James Monroe Watson

James Monroe "Jim" Watson was born in eastern Tennessee in 1834, the eldest of twelve children who survived to adulthood. He left Tennessee with his family in 1848, aiming for Texas. After a journey that required the best part of two years, they arrived in Rusk County, Texas.

As the oldest child, Jim played a significant role in developing the new family farm and building a two-room log home for his parents and boisterous siblings. As was often the pattern on the American frontier, the Watsons began organizing a church and school as soon as their farm was working.

Twenty-six years old when Lincoln was elected, Watson, like his father and family, opposed secession, not being slaveowners themselves. Nevertheless, Texas voted to secede and join the Confederacy. When war broke out in April of 1861, he laid aside his opposition to secession and joined the Confederate Army, serving in Company G of the Tenth Texas Cavalry.

The oldest two of Watson's younger brothers joined as well, and they went east with the army to Mississippi. The two younger brothers both died of disease in camp, before they ever saw action. Watson's first detail involved bringing his unit's horses back to Texas. The army had too much cavalry, and the horses were needed on the home front.

He managed to cross the Mississippi with the horses and delivered them successfully back home, then made his way back to his unit. The Union army invaded Arkansas while he was on the road, and he was diverted northward to join the defense. Following the Confederate defeat at the Battle of Pea Ridge, he resumed his journey to the east to rejoin the Tenth Texas.

Watson was shot through the abdomen at the Battle of Chickamauga, so severely wounded that he was left for dead on the field. His best friend from home braved enemy gunfire to retrieve him, and brought him back to the aid station. The friend soaked his silk handkerchief in whiskey and stuffed it into Watson's wound with his musket's ramrod, Watson lay outside the aid station all night, untreated. In the morning, finding him still alive, the medics finally dealt with his injury.

After six months of recovery, he rejoined the army and served until the end of the war. He refused to wait to be paroled by the Union authorities. Parole was for criminals, he reasoned, and he was no criminal for defending his State from invasion. So it was he walked back from southern Alabama to Rusk County, Texas, in 1865.

Watson settled once again on the family land in East Texas, building his own cabin, marrying, and having children. His daughter remembered that he had one scar on his stomach where the musket ball entered his body, and two on his back. The bullet had split in two inside him, thus missing his spine and allowing him to live.

Because he had refused a federal parole, he was never eligible in old age for the small pension Texas paid to its Confederate veterans. He died in 1914, surrounded by his children and grandchildren.

Watson's decision to fight shows the complexity of the Civil War era. As an opponent of both secession and slavery, he chose to fight in defense of his home, family, and State, not to perpetuate the terrible injustice so widely practiced at the time.

Nathan Bedford Forrest

Nathan Bedford Forrest was born in rural Tennessee in 1821. Like Abraham Lincoln, he grew up in what later generations would have considered abject poverty. His father died while Forrest was still a youth, leaving him to provide for his family. Also like Lincoln, Forrest rose by dint of formidable talent, determination, and ambition to the heights of success in his State, without the benefit of formal schooling.

By the late 1850s, Forrest had amassed great wealth for the time, owning cotton plantations and trading in livestock and, more lucratively, enslaved humans. He was reportedly the richest man in Tennessee when war broke out in 1861.

Despite his wealth, Forrest enlisted as a private in the Confederate States Army when the war began. Shortly thereafter, though, Tennessee's governor asked him to raise and supply a cavalry unit. He did so and was commissioned as a lieutenant colonel. He served thereafter with a relentless and impatient brilliance.

In April of 1864, Forrest's command besieged a small Union garrison at Fort Pillow, Tennessee. When the garrison refused to surrender, Forrest ordered his troops to attack. They did so, overwhelming the predominantly Black garrison in bitter combat. In the heat of the battle, with command and control breaking down, Forrest's troops massacred many of the Black soldiers as they attempted to surrender. Forrest denied vehemently that he had commanded such actions, though a U. S. Congressional investigation held him responsible.

He rose to the rank of lieutenant general by the end of the war, his cavalry tactics having caused tremendous delay and destruction to the ongoing Union onslaught in the Western Theater. In the end, of course, it was not enough. A month after being defeated at the Battle of Selma, Alabama, in April, 1865, he surrendered his command and laid down his arms.

Returning to Tennessee after the war, Forrest helped organize what he intended to be a white, self-defense militia to resist the chaos of the time. In the defeated South, the militia had to keep its membership hidden from the Union Army to avoid arrest and open conflict. This group, which called itself the Ku Klux Klan, elected Forrest as its first Grand Wizard in 1867. Forrest's fame gave the organization wide influence among aggrieved Southern whites.

Yet Forrest, disgusted by the violence the Klan unleashed, ordered the organization to disband in 1869 and attempted to move away from it. His fortune destroyed by the war, he started over from scratch thereafter.

According to many who knew him, Forrest became a changed man late in life. Through his wife's influence, he came to faith in Jesus Christ, joined the church, stopped drinking and swearing, and sought to make amends with the Black community. In 1874, after the lynching of four Black Americans by a white mob, Forrest volunteered his services to hunt down the perpetrators. Tennessee's governor declined his offer.

In 1875, in one of the most surprising moments of his life, an unarmed, unaccompanied Forrest addressed a substantial gathering of Black Americans at a convention in Nashville. He publicly professed his love for them and his concern for their ongoing advancement. At the end of the speech, he was presented with flowers by a young Black woman. To the great disgust of many of his white compatriots, he thanked her and kissed her on the cheek.

In a subsequent speech to a Black barbecue gathering in Memphis, he urged his hearers to "work, be industrious, live honestly, and act truly." He then declared that "when you are oppressed, I'll come to your relief."

Consumed by diabetes, he died in October of 1877 in Memphis.

Former Confederate President Jefferson Davis lamented late in life that he had been too slow in recognizing Forrest's military genius. Forrest became a symbol of resistance to many Southern whites, and of violent racism to many Blacks. He was undoubtedly a sworn enemy of Liberty for much of his life. Whether his late conversion to Christ and repentance should be laid in the balance to his credit is something for others to decide.

Elijah Adams

Elijah Adams, who adopted the surname of his former 'owners' after gaining freedom, was born sometime around 1810 on a cotton plantation in Georgia. By the standards other enslaved persons faced, his treatment was relatively mild.

Adams was a field hand, his work following the rhythm of the seasons. His enslavers provided sufficient food and adequate shelter. He was allowed to marry, and the children he fathered were not sold away.

When the war broke out, Adams was already on the edge of being considered old by the standards of field hands. His hands were calloused and rough, as were his feet. He had never worn shoes in his life.

The plantation where he lived was in the path of Sherman's army after the Battle of Atlanta, and the main house and outbuildings were burned to the ground by Union soldiers. What food stores the troops did not take were destroyed in the fires. Those soldiers announced to the two hundred or so enslaved souls gathered there that they were free, then moved on. Many followed them, and others drifted away, all trying to find their bearings in newfound Liberty.

Adams refused to leave. He was too old, he said, to keep up. Instead, he and his wife remained in a cabin on the ruined property. After a difficult winter struggling to find food in the denuded countryside, the Adams put in a crop the following year and resumed their agricultural life.

They settled into a sharecropping arrangement with the property's impoverished white 'owners.' As age took further hold, one of his daughters took him into her care. He died in 1885 in the same place he had lived all his life.

Erna Beth Adams

Erna Beth Adams was born sometime in the late 1820s on the Georgia plantation where her future husband Elijah was enslaved. She worked in the "Big House," cooking, cleaning, and taking care of the white family's children and grandchildren.

She and Elijah married in the early 1840s when she was hardly more than a child. Her new husband terrified her at first, with his huge calloused hands and gruff manner. Yet he won her over with his unexpected gentleness, both with her and with the eight children they had together.

When the tide of war swept over their home and left much of it in smoking ruins, she and Elijah decided to stay where they were and rebuild. It took eighteen months of enormous effort, scavenging, bartering, trapping small game, and, sometimes, just going hungry, to get through until their first postwar crop came in. At that point, the constant hunger they had come to know eased.

With the "Big House" destroyed and the whites as impoverished as the Blacks, Erna Beth scrambled to find a living while simple Elijah continued his daily work in the fields. She sewed, baked, kept house for herself and others, and raised the community's children, both white and Black, to make ends meet. A new semblance of normal emerged, though, in the years that followed.

She assumed greater and greater shares of the burden as Elijah aged out of the ability to contribute. Nevertheless, she remained faithfully at his side until his death. Thereafter, she moved in with a nearby daughter, where she remained until her death in 1899.

Liberty for Erna Beth Adams meant a profound struggle for survival, followed by years of incessant labor. As she neared the end, she found herself at peace with the reality of being able to lay down her burdens in death.

Willis Hinton

Willis Hinton, enslaved in North Carolina, managed logistics for field hands working on several plantations nearby. His 'owners' had discovered his talents when he was a young boy and put them to full use.

He never learned to read or write, but arranged daily food and seasonal work cycles using his prodigious memory and an attention to detail. When freedom came, he settled not far from his home county in a place largely untouched by the physical destruction of the war.

There, he went into business for himself, building a thriving general store in his community. He was successful by reading people and faces, rather than papers. His genial nature made others naturally inclined to trust him, but underneath was a shrewd businessman who had no tolerance for cheaters and thieves.

He died in 1877.

Benjamin "Pap" Singleton

Benjamin "Pap" Singleton was born in Davidson County, northern Tennessee, in 1809. At age 37, Singleton managed to escape his captors and flee to Ontario, Canada.

He returned from Canada prior to the outbreak of the Civil War, settling in Detroit. There, he became a noted abolitionist, anxious for both the freedom and well-being of his people.

When war broke out, Singleton returned to Tennessee with the Union occupation, helping literally hundreds of the formerly enslaved escape to freedom. After the war ended, he watched in growing disillusionment as the fruits of Liberty were snatched away from the newly freed by resurgent white racism and violence.

In response, Singleton began urging Blacks to leave the defeated South. He organized the movement of hundreds into Kansas, where they gathered into communities of their own, not under the thumbs of white control. He advocated for Black businesses and education.

As the postwar period progressed, Singleton began to advocate Black nationalism and toyed with the idea of a mass movement back to Africa, convinced that permanent progress would be impossible in the United States. Liberty, he concluded, was a tree that would not grow for Black folk in the harsh soil of America.

He earned the nickname "Pap" for his tireless efforts to help others first to freedom and then to independence and self-sufficiency. He died in Kansas City, Missouri, in 1900.

Al Smith

Al Smith grew up enslaved on a horse ranch in central Texas, reaching adulthood around the time the war broke out. Federal troops withdrew from Texas at that point, and most able-bodied white male Texans left to fight.

The situation in central Texas became grave. Emboldened by the sudden absence of both Federal troops and local males, the Comanche and others intensified their raids against settlers. They burned outlying ranches and massacred the whites who fell into their hands, pushing the frontier in Texas back over a hundred miles as the war raged.

Smith, as a Black man, was left untouched by the Indian onslaught. For the first and only time in his life, the color of his skin worked to his advantage. He drifted through the chaos of the settlements, continuing to make his living working with horses. He was never formally "freed;" the institution of slavery simply crumbled around him where he was.

When the war ended, the U. S. Army and the surviving Confederate veterans returned. After securing the Rio Grande border with cavalry, Union General Philip "Little Phil" Sheridan waged war against the Comanche with all the skills and firepower learned in the late combat to the east.

Smith, with his horses, drifted onto the plains, where he became part of the pioneering generation of cowboys. On horseback, driving cattle north to Kansas, skin color mattered far less than hard work and perseverance. He found his Liberty, like many other Black cowboys, in the saddle and on the trail.

John Henry Smith

John Henry Smith was born in 1848, just off the military road that ran through Pike County, Alabama, near the young city of Troy. South Alabama was a haven for "fire-breathers," those who passionately favored secession and war.

In the aftermath of Lincoln's election, the region was a whirlwind of fervent activity. Alabama was one of the seven States to originally secede, and Montgomery, fifty miles up the road, was the first Confederate capital.

John Henry Smith, age twelve, watched enviously as his older brother and many neighbors joined the Confederate army and marched off to what all were sure would be a quick, victorious war.

Three years later, after Shiloh, after Vicksburg, after Gettysburg, the well of young Southern men for the grinding conflict was running dry. Much less envious now at fifteen, mindful of grieving families nearby, he enlisted, becoming what is now called a child soldier.

His first action was the horrific slaughter at Franklin, Tennessee. Stupefied by terror, he went forward with his unit in Hood's foolish headlong assault. A volley from the Union breastworks struck down four men to his left at once. A slug of grapeshot decapitated his unit's sergeant on his right. John Henry crumpled to the ground among the twitching corpses, unhurt but too terrified to move.

Eventually night fell and the thunder of battle eased. All he could hear were the moans of the wounded and the shrieks of dying men and horses. He lay There, covered in others' blood, surrounded by a lifeless pile of mangled flesh. At some point in the darkness, he got up and staggered into the nearby woods, away from the terrible open field littered with death.

For three days he drifted through the thickets as if in a nightmare, until he was taken prisoner by a Union patrol. He spent the rest of the war in a prison camp. From the moment of his capture, he lived with terrible shame at what he believed was his cowardice.

Night after night, starting in the prison camp, he dreamed he was again on the battlefield amidst the carnage. He would wake screaming, drenched in sweat. In the camp, no one seemed to notice, gripped as all were in their own terror.

John Henry Smith returned to Polk County, Alabama, when the war ended. He found his childhood home destroyed, his family gone without a trace. He noticed in the years that followed how much others delighted in telling war stories, especially, it seemed, those who hadn't served. Somehow, he could never bring himself to say a word.

Alton Beard

Alton Beard was born enslaved to a family of pig farmers in the rich, alluvial plain along the Mississippi in southeastern Missouri. His life moved with the cycle of the rooting beasts.

When the secession crisis hit and the war came, all of Missouri was convulsed. The legislature refused to secede, but the larger part of the citizens sympathized with the Confederacy. In that environment, Confederate General Sterling Price led a desperate effort to conquer the State and secure the vital port at Saint Louis.

It did not succeed. Union Commander Nathaniel Lyon set out in pursuit of the Confederate-aligned State militia and Price's outnumbered forces. Though the Union held the State, guerilla leaders like William Quantrill and William Anderson began a reign of terror behind the lines. Young Jesse James learned his brutal trade under Anderson beginning in 1864.

In the chaos, Beard escaped his captors. Traveling by night through the thickets along the Mississippi, he headed north, avoiding settlements. After a brief sojourn in Saint Louis, he set out again. Both the bloodlust of the southern sympathizers and the demands of the Union war machine spurred him on.

He found refuge in a quiet spot near Bethany, in the far northwest of the State. In the hollow of a creek bed there, he found a sounder of pigs, escapees like himself from captivity elsewhere. He cautiously trapped a few and began to do what he had done all his life.

Beard worried for years that someone would come along and eject him from the pig farm he began to build for himself there, but no one ever did. He eventually married, put up a house and barn, and raised a family.

Liberty for Alton Beard was a pig farm of his own, free from Liberty-denying taskmasters.

Jerry Atkins

Jerry Atkins escaped slavery as a young man in northern Virginia in the late 1850s. He made his way to the safe haven of Massachusetts, where he lived for many years.

Long after the war ended, he returned to his Virginia birthplace. Needless to say, he found it radically transformed. The farm he had grown up on had changed hands many times, divided among strangers.

With fear and trembling, he looked up the family who had 'owned' him prior to his escape. He found the wife of his former master, old, impoverished, and bedbound in the home of a daughter.

After introducing himself downstairs to the daughter, he asked to see the old woman. Admitted into her presence, he introduced himself again. At first, she didn't know him, but soon he saw the light of recognition in her eyes. To his amazement and delight, it was a recognition of love and not reproach.

"Jerry," she said through tears of joy, "is that you?"

"Yes, ma'am," he answered.

She sobbed, "Oh Jerry, my husband's gone. It's all gone."

"Yes, ma'am," he answered again. "But you're here with your daughter now, and she loves you."

"Jerry," she said almost in shock, "you've become such a gentleman!"

"I always was, ma'am."

He settled nearby, finding work and sharing voluntarily in the old woman's care until she died. Somehow, their shared traumas bound them together in forgiving love after all the years.

When Jerry grew old and unable to care for himself, the grandchildren of those who once claimed to 'own' him took care of him in turn. He died in his own bed, surrounded by loved ones both Black and white.

In Jerry Atkins' living and dying, Liberty was perfected in love.

James Beckwourth

James Beckwourth was born into slavery around 1800 in Virginia, a son of his 'owner.' His father freed him in adolescence and apprenticed him to a blacksmith to learn a trade.

Beckwourth blacksmithed his way west through the years, his trade connecting him with fur trappers and traders, among others. Eventually, Beckwourth himself became a pioneer trapper and mountain man in the Rockies.

He lived among the Crow Nation for a while, discovering while with them the lowest pass through the Sierra Nevadas. His was the first trail opened through that mountain range, from Reno, Nevada, to California. By chance, the great California Gold Rush broke out in 1849, and Beckwourth's trail became quite important.

Beckwourth built a rugged hotel alongside the trail and regaled travelers who stopped for the night with stories of his adventures in the mountains. He dictated his life story, full of often-hilarious and often-impossible tall tales, to a passing journalist.

The broad outlines of his life needed no exaggeration, though. He blazed a trail from slavery in Virginia to Liberty in the Rockies, opening a road for the original "49ers."

Beckwourth died in 1866 near Fort Smith, Montana.

Ginny Scott

Ginny Scott was her family's first college graduate after liberation. She joined Liberty's dance in 1866, born to parents who fled wartime chaos in northern Mississippi and found shelter in central Ohio.

Before she became the first college graduate, she was also the first child in her family with access to public education at all. Teaching Black children to read and write had been illegal in the slave State of her birth.

The child was bright and inquisitive, and her teachers helped her make the most of it. In 1882, she enrolled at Wilberforce College, not far from her home. Wilberforce itself, founded in 1837 as the nation's first Black college, had been run since 1862 by the African Methodist Episcopal Church.

Ginny became a teacher after graduation and remained in the profession for life. For two generations, she did for other children what others had done for her. Over the decades, she taught thousands of Black children in Cincinnati.

She died in 1908, never having married. Though she had no children of her own, hundreds of her former students filled Allen Temple African Methodist Episcopal Church in Cincinatti for her funeral.

Many of Liberty's heroes before and since have been teachers.

Bridget "Biddy" Mason

Bridget "Biddy" Mason was born enslaved in 1818 in Mississippi. Her 'owner' converted to Mormonism when she was a young woman and decided to move west with all his household to the Mormon mecca of Utah.

So it happened that Biddy, aged 30, walked 1,700 miles from Mississippi to Utah behind the enslaver's wagon train in 1848. She carried three daughters with her on the journey, aged 10, 4, and a newborn.

After several years in Utah, the same 'owner' decided to move to California. California, however, took a dim view of slavery. By law, it only allowed slaveholders a temporary residence before forcing them to either free those they enslaved or leave.

Biddy's 'owner' feared losing his slaves and decided to move to Texas. Biddy Mason challenged him in court under California law in 1856 and won. She was freed along with her family and decided to stay in California.

She became a landowner in Los Angeles thereafter and one of the most prominent early Black residents of the city. She played a key role in establishing the First African Methodist Episcopal Church of Los Angeles in 1871.

Mason died in 1891 and, despite relative prominence in her community, was buried in an unmarked grave. More than a century later, mindful of her historic role, the people of Los Angeles corrected this slight by putting up a marker and monument to her.

Biddy Mason's life testifies to the transforming power of Liberty in law, and to those with the fortitude necessary to challenge injustice by it.

George Washington Carver

George Washington Carver was born in Diamond, Missouri, in 1864, during the last gasps of slavery. Lincoln's Emancipation Proclamation had freed those enslaved in the States in rebellion. Because Missouri had not seceded, those enslaved within it remained in bondage until the State abolished the practice in January of 1865.

At the age of one week, newborn George was kidnapped along with his mother and brother by one of the gangs of Confederate raiders who terrorized Missouri during the war. George's 'owner,' Moses Carver, hired a man to track them down, but George alone was found. Along with his brother, George was raised in the Carver home thereafter as one of the family's own children.

The local school in Diamond, Missouri, wouldn't admit George as a student because of his skin color. With the Carvers' blessing, he went to the 'big city' of Neosho, Missouri, ten miles away, to enroll instead. George was a brilliant student and a magnetic personality. He developed a specialty in botany, and in 1891 became the first Black student to enroll at Iowa State University.

Invited to teach at Tuskegee Institute in Alabama, he began his work there in 1896. While at Tuskegee, he pioneered the practice of crop rotation to restore farmland depleted by the growth of cotton. He also advanced and diversified the production of peanuts.

Carver was one of the first Black Americans to offer expert testimony to the U. S. Congress, despite mockery from many Southern lawmakers. President Theodore Roosevelt publicly admired his work, and the Royal Society of Arts in England made him one of its few American members in 1916.

As his fame grew, Carver devoted himself to the uplift of his people and to racial reconciliation. He toured Southern colleges for the Commission on Interracial Cooperation during the 1920s and 1930s. Carver met three U. S. presidents during his lifetime, and taught a special three-week course on agronomy to the Crown Prince of Sweden.

He never married and died in 1943 after suffering a bad fall. The epitaph on his gravestone reads, "He could have added fortune to fame, but caring for neither, he found happiness and honor in being helpful to the world."

His towering intellect is a monument in the cause of Liberty.

John D Rockefeller

John D. Rockefeller came into the world in 1839, in Richford, New York. His mother was a devout Baptist who instilled her faith, diligence, and sense of obligation in her son. His father was a flamboyant traveling salesman, rarely at home and only a distant presence in the lives of his children.

The young Rockefeller showed an early aptitude for business and began building his holdings with a tremendous eye for detail and organization. He grasped how important oil was becoming to the larger economy and set his sights on its exploitation. By the time the Civil War broke out, he had already amassed a respectable fortune. He hired a substitute to take his place in the army.

The war intensified the transition toward oil, and Rockefeller multiplied his business interests and wealth. Fully aware of the cyclical nature of energy demands, he husbanded resources during flush times and bought out his competitors during downturns.

By the 1880s, he controlled 90% of oil output in the United States, firmly ensconced on the towering heights of the American economy. His great wealth and power aroused bitter opposition among former rivals, as well as increasing suspicion and hostility in government and public opinion.

The opprobrium heaped on him in the press and in public hurt him emotionally, but didn't stop him from pursuing his purposes. The federal government, created to oversee an agrarian republic, lacked effective tools to confront monopolies at the time. The labor movement then emerging struggled to counter the power of the era's predatory capitalism.

By the end of the 1880s, Rockefeller was the nation's first billionaire, his business interests spanning the country and crossing the globe. He began moving toward retirement in the 1890s, settling in Kykuit, a mansion he had built in Westchester County, New York.

As the 20th Century dawned, the federal government began to develop tools for curbing the power of massive trusts like Rockefeller's, and labor unions grew in effectiveness. By this point, Rockefeller's own attentions were turning toward philanthropy.

True to his precise nature, he funded significant medical research, insisting on verifiable, evidence-based results. He used his wealth to found universities in the United States and in the Philippines, then an American possession. The University of Chicago, which he founded, grew into one of the nation's finest.

Through it all, Rockefeller remained a devout, church-going Baptist. He taught Sunday School, supported church-based institutions, and was a lifelong teetotaler who abstained from tobacco as well. He was well aware of the contrast between his pious personal life and the occasional brutality of the businesses he controlled, and shrewd enough to realize that much of it was beyond his control, even with all his wealth and power.

As he aged, he never lost interest either in his philanthropy or his business. Spurred by federal antitrust statutes, he successfully split his trust into manageable entities, passing on a vast inheritance to his heirs. As an old man in the early years of the Great Depression, he kept a stock of dimes with him at all times and was noted for giving them away to people he met on the street.

Rockefeller died at age 97, in 1937, survived by his five children. He wielded his Liberty ruthlessly in the eyes of many, but ethically according to his own standards. His contributions to the world's well-being through his scientific philanthropy are ongoing.

Claude McKay

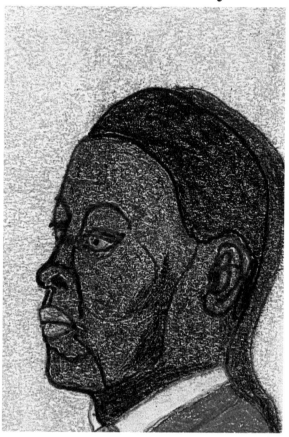

Festus Claudius McKay, known as Claude, came into the world on the island of Jamaica in 1889, born among the Black Baptist communities there who had played such a crucial role in Britain's 1834 abolition of slavery. His parents were prosperous, having amassed enough land that Claude's father qualified to vote.

Claude's parents apprenticed him as a woodworker, but his real interests were literary. Tutored by an older brother who was a teacher and an English-born neighbor with an excellent library, young McKay sated himself on great English authors and continental philosophy.

Having won an award in Jamaica for his early poetry, he financed a voyage to America, intending to study at Tuskegee Institute. The virulent racism he encountered disembarking in Charleston, South Carolina, shocked him. He detested the militaristic program he found at Tuskegee and left after two months, enrolling instead at Kansas State College (later University).

McKay left college completely in 1914, migrating to New York and supporting himself with a succession of menial jobs. The racism he encountered drove him to write, and his most famous poem, "If We Must Die," was published to some recognition there in 1919.

McKay's experiences of ongoing oppression drove him to the radical left at the time. He became an atheist and communist after the style of Vladimir Lenin's Bolsheviks, at least in theory. He lived for a while in England, writing for radical publications and skating on the edge of legal trouble for his views.

Invited to the Soviet Union, he attended the Communist International meeting there in 1924. He wrote two works there on the Black experience in America, both of which were translated into Russian. Later on, he acknowledged that he only saw in Russia those things his handlers wanted him to see.

After a stint in Paris, McKay returned to New York. The so-called "Harlem Renaissance" was blossoming, and he played a key role in it as one of its earliest and most radical voices. Yet his involvement with the New York Communist Party became problematic as Stalin rose to power. The party's New York leader was a Stalinist. McKay was not.

McKay's writing portrayed Black life in much of its variety. He resisted presenting only idealized portraits, provoking criticism from other writers who accused him of undermining his own community. Communists attacked him for supporting civil rights and racial solidarity, rather than violent revolution.

McKay became a U. S. citizen in 1940. The longtime atheist converted to Catholicism in 1942, won from his militant unbelief by a loving community that ministered to him. He spent the rest of his days working with Catholic youth, dying in 1948 in Chicago.

Claude McKay, descendant of those who triggered the liberation of millions, gamely described the state of Liberty as he saw it, regardless of the consequences. He himself lived with sufficient Liberty to be changed late in life by unexpected love and faith.

John L Sullivan

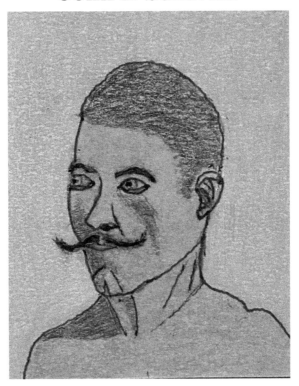

John Lawrence Sullivan, son of Irish immigrants, was born in the Boston area in 1858. A gifted athlete, Sullivan enrolled briefly at Boston College before leaving to pursue his athletic dreams.

After turning down an offer to play professional baseball, he focused on boxing. Boxing at the time was far more brutal than it is now. Fighters often engaged in bare-knuckle bouts that would last dozens of rounds, until one or both fighters could go no further. Because of boxing's brutality, it was illegal in many jurisdictions, and matches often had to be arranged in secret.

Sullivan's heavyweight title, won in 1882, was the last one won under bare-knuckle rules. In 1889, he defended his title in the final bare-knuckle championship bout, which lasted a staggering seventy-five (75) rounds.

Sullivan had a huge personality to go with his enormous strength, and drank heavily throughout his boxing career. He married young, left his wife for an exotic dancer, and then abandoned her to marry his childhood sweetheart, Kate Harkins, in 1883. Under Kate's influence, he eventually gave up alcohol and became an advocate for temperance.

Sullivan won an estimated $1 million in prize money during his boxing career, a huge sum for the day. He seems to have spent it all in riotous living before being reformed by his third wife.

Sullivan died in 1918, having been perhaps the first in a long line of America's celebrity athletes. Liberty for this son of Irish immigrants led to fame, brutality, dissipation, and, at least in some eyes, redemption.

"Blind Tom" Wiggins

Thomas Greene Wiggins was born into slavery on a Georgia plantation in 1849. As an infant, he was sold with his parents to a Georgia newspaper editor, General James Bethune. Bethune's newspaper was among the first to advocate secession in the South.

Blind from birth, Tom accompanied his mother as she performed household tasks for the Bethunes. After hearing the white children during a piano lesson one day in the home, Tom went to the piano and replicated everything he had heard by ear. Astounded, the Bethunes subsequently arranged lessons for the child and gave him free access to the piano.

His musical genius manifested itself quickly. General Bethune, his 'owner,' sensing an opportunity for profit, began to arrange concerts for the child. By 1860, "Blind Tom," as he became known, was among the most famous musicians in the country. He became that year the first Black American to entertain at the White House, playing for President James Buchanan.

Tom seems to have been autistic as well as blind, though the term was unknown at the time. When the war ended and liberation came, General Bethune manipulated the laws to have himself declared Tom's permanent guardian. This enabled him to continue promoting Tom's performances and allowed him to keep the profits generated by them.

Tom performed throughout the United States and toured Europe, wowing audiences everywhere he went. No less an eminence than Mark Twain attended three consecutive nights of Tom's performances, according to the White House Historical Association.

After continuous legal challenges to his white guardians, they withdrew him from the performing circuit in the last years of the 1890s. Tom was settled under their care in New Jersey. He died after suffering a stroke in 1908.

Despite the apparent triumph of Liberty at Emancipation, "Blind Tom" Wiggins, because of his disabilities and the avarice of his wards, never seems to have experienced it.

William Casby

William Casby was born into slavery in Danville, Virginia, in 1857. Liberated by the Union victory, Casby lived long enough to see both Reconstruction and the Civil Rights Movement.

Life eventually took him to Algiers, Louisiana, where he was photographed and interviewed by the famous American photographer Richard Avedon. Despite the struggles of a long lifetime, Casby stated, "I know changes have happened; they will happen again... I believe things will be better."

He died in 1970, aged 113, having held his great-great-grandchildren in his arms.

Lila Johnson

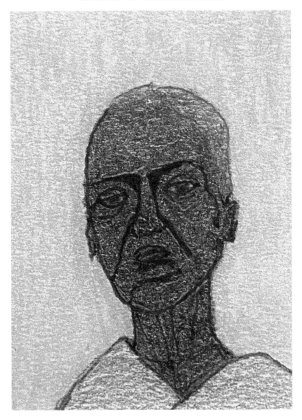

Lila Johnson came into the world in slavery in Arkansas around the year 1850. She was one of a handful of enslaved persons belonging to a small family of farmers, a hundred miles or so west of the Mississippi. A child when war broke out, she and the others felt giddy that freedom might be near.

Union forces invaded Arkansas in 1862, systematically stripping the land they occupied of anything that could be of use to the rebels: livestock, food stores, and enslaved humans. At one point, the Union army got close enough that Lila could hear the distant sounds of gunfire. She watched the endless wagon trains of supplies going north to the front and the same wagons coming south, full of the wounded.

Yet freedom wasn't at hand. Her 'owners' decided to flee south, taking their livestock and humans with them into the deep woods of northern Louisiana. They remained there for the rest of the war, out of reach of the liberating army but facing increasing hunger. Lila detested cornbread for the rest of her life, since that was often all she and those with her had to eat during those lean years.

Freedom didn't come until the war ended, when Union occupiers compelled the remaining slave owners to set their captives free. By then a young woman of childbearing age, Lila was given the opportunity to either stay and work for pay or leave. She and two others left immediately.

They settled in Shreveport's freedman's town. She married twice. Her first husband abandoned her, and the second was killed in a drunken brawl. Along the way, she gave birth to six children. Given no choice in the matter, Lila toiled without opportunity for rest for the remainder of her days.

As an old woman, she looked back with a measure of nostalgia for her childhood, when someone else made all the decisions and there was at least time to play. Liberty was real for Lila, but for reasons beyond her control, it seemed less free than the life she had known before.

Clara Brim

U. S. President Franklin D. Roosevelt launched the Federal Writers' Project in 1935 during the depths of the Great Depression as a way to both provide work for unemployed writers and to document aspects of America's living history. One of the Project's projects was the Slave Narrative Project, intended to capture some of the stories of freed men and women who remained alive at the time.

Clara Brim's was one such story. She joined Liberty's dance around 1835, born into slavery on a plantation owned by William Lyons in Plaquemine Bouley, Acadia, Louisiana. Clara's life in slavery was relatively benign by the standards of the time.

Lyons provided decent housing with real fireplaces, she recalled. He would typically assign his slaves one task each week. When they completed it, they were free to work for pay for others. There was food and medical care, and Lyons allowed a weekly church service and a minister on call for emergencies.

When the war came, one of Brim's brothers was sent away. She never saw him again. Nevertheless, she chose to remain with Lyons after liberation, working for pay. When her husband died in 1913, she moved in with a daughter in Beaumont, Texas, where she remained for the rest of her life.

The Writers' Project caught up with her in 1937. She was still active, still helping to keep house at the age of around 102. Her hope at the time was for a better life for her grandchildren and great-grandchildren.

Mary Estelle

Mary Estelle always carried herself with the genteel mannerisms she had learned as a girl working in the "Big House." Underneath the veneer, though, was a woman scarred by terror and trauma.

Born into slavery in the early 1840s on a large plantation in Georgia, she had fine features as a child. Her 'owners' brought her inside the house when she was hardly more than six to teach her to sew: fine fabrics for the whites, coarse ones for the Blacks.

She lived in an atmosphere of tension from the beginning. The plantation's overseer, a cruel man, maintained a harsh order with the whip. Mary saw small infractions earn painful punishments and learned to stay as quiet as she could to avoid attracting attention.

Twin events when she was around eight seared themselves into her mind. One blustery afternoon, the 'master' gathered the enslaved together to show them all to a younger cousin who was moving to Texas to start a plantation there. The older people understood what was coming, but Mary had no clue.

The cousin examined the 'property' closely, then pointed his finger at Mary's mother and two older sisters. The 'Master' sold them on the spot as Mary stood there in wordless shock. Later that afternoon, the young cousin loaded the three into a wagon and disappeared down the road. Mary never saw them again.

A few weeks later, Mary heard a commotion in the yard outside the slave quarters. She ran out to see the overseer strapping one of the field hands, a younger man she had known all her life, to a tree. The field hand had talked back to him, and he intended to make an example of him. She and the others watched in horror as the Black man was beaten to death before their eyes. The overseer left his body tied to the tree for days to "teach 'em all a lesson."

When she was hardly more than fourteen, the master's second son noticed her fine features while she worked. The white youth was loud and entitled, fond of racing horses and terrorizing the neighborhood. He raped her for the first time on the floor of the sewing room.

The assaults continued for several years. She gave birth to two children as a result, both chattel like herself. She never managed to feel any warmth toward them because of the memories, only able to mother them coldly.

When the war came, this brash second son enlisted and marched away as an officer. When word came he had been killed at Shiloh, Mary's heart was stone cold amidst the grief of her white 'owners.'

After freedom, she settled in nearby Natchez, finding steady work as a seamstress. The children drifted away as soon as they were able. She made no effort to hold them back.

Mary lived to old age in Natchez, elegantly dressed by her own hands, elegantly mannered, yet utterly shut off from a world that had long ago left her broken inside. Liberty for her was just another meaningless word.

"Old Man" Elkins

"Old Man" Elkins started his life over on the western frontier after the War Between the States. There were fewer questions that way for one who had ridden with William Quantrill in Missouri.

He set out for the high plains with a horse, a length of rope, a saddle, and a bag of tools. He built up a herd at the beginning by rounding up wild longhorn cattle whose ancestors had long ago escaped from Spanish corrals.

At no small personal risk, he and others pioneered a beef industry that soon fed much of the nation. It was grueling work, leading herds from grazing grounds in Texas to railheads in Kansas for shipment east. There was no law on the trail, and very little in the towns. Hostile Indians still roamed the plains. The cowboy lifestyle, much romanticized later, hardened those who survived it, and Elkins was no exception.

He lived long enough to see the partial pacification of the Indian tribes his work helped dispossess. The years and hard labor took their toll, though, and he retired to the edge of a small town in the Texas panhandle.

Elkins was a solitary old man without family or friends when he died in 1883. No one living near him at the time ever remembered hearing his first name.

Fanny Moore

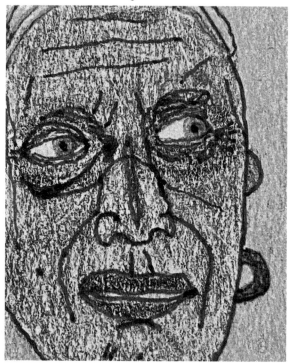

Fanny Moore was born into slavery in the late 1850s in the Shenandoah Valley of Virginia. Her earliest memories were of columns of gray-clad troops marching up the road, followed by long lines of wagons.

She was around eight when the tide of war shifted against her 'owners' in the Valley. She remembered waking up one morning to the shouts of 'Ol' Miss,' her 'owner's' wife. Fanny ran outside, where her mother grabbed her by the hand and held her close.

The ol' miss stood before a man in a blue uniform, screaming at him, "You can't do that! They belong to me!"

The man in blue laughed in her face. She remembered him saying, "Not anymore they don't."

Then, as she watched with shocked eyes, other men in blue set fire to the 'Master's' house. The old white lady screamed and screamed, but it made no difference. As the flames consumed the house, the first man turned to the Black faces gathered around and said, "You people is free. You ain't gotta do nothin' this old hag tells you any more!"

The old woman stood there in stunned silence. Eventually, the men in blue went away, and she turned to Fanny's mother. "Dear, go get me a glass of water," she said.

Fanny's mother didn't move, her face frozen.

The white woman spoke again, her shrill voice rising, "Go get me some water, I said!"

Fanny's mother's lips curled into a snarl. "I ain't gonna do it," she roared back. "That man said I didn't have to, and I ain't gonna do it!"

The old lady stood there, stunned. Fanny's mother turned her back, still holding her daughter's hand, and walked away.

For the rest of Fanny's life, Liberty was a defiant snarl against those who no longer could give her orders.

Tillie Johnson

Tillie Johnson came into the world in 1866, born to a family of white landowners. They had made their living alongside enslaved labor prior to the war and went through wrenching changes along with the Black population in the years immediately after it.

Tillie's family owned the land, but lacked the labor to work it themselves after liberation. The Blacks had been freed, but there had been no land reform with their Liberty. Carpetbagger politicians promised them the mythical "forty acres and a mule," but never delivered on the promise.

Various solutions followed. Tillie's family settled on sharecropping agreements with many of the free Blacks living nearby. Where sharecroppers were unavailable, they either left the land fallow or, if taxes were too high, sold it to newcomers.

She was a child when her family moved into town. Her father developed a farm implement business that kept them fed and looked after their rural interests. Her mother raised the children, focused on running her household in reduced circumstances. Tillie and her sisters enrolled in the local public school.

According to the practice of the time, white children were only educated with other white children and taught only by white teachers. The "colored" children went to a different school entirely, and Tillie had next to no interaction with them. She assumed growing up that was the way things always had been and always would be.

Reconstruction ended during her teen years, and the white power structure rolled back the civil rights the Black community had briefly tasted. Since it did not impact her directly, she was largely unaware of it.

Tillie and her peers shared a deep-seated, at times irrational fear of Black violence, as had their forebears before them. Politicians stirred that pot often, manipulating it in the name of segregating white folks from dangers real and imagined.

Throughout her life, relations with Black people were transactional. Her family paid Blacks for their labor either in cash or with crops, sold them farm implements when they had money to buy them, and nodded politely when they passed on the street. The Blacks, of course, were expected to step aside to let them pass. Other than those moments, they had no social interaction of consequence.

She died in 1956 at age 89. Those who gathered at her funeral and graveside service were all white. A Black crew dug the grave and lowered the casket into it once the mourners had gone.

Presley Campbell

The white folks said that Presley Campbell, born to a newly freed couple near Malakoff, Texas, came into this world with a smile on his face. In part, it was true. The child was blessed with a sunny disposition and an optimistic outlook his whole life. In part, of course, it was not.

Presley's parents rode out the spasm of violence that followed the Civil War in eastern Texas. They saw the barbaric law the masked white men dealt so easily to Blacks who crossed them. They raised Presley to remember that a cross word, a casual look, could unleash such violence on a Black man, whether deserved or not. He took the lesson to heart.

In fact, life seemed to smile on his family as the region recovered. They sharecropped farmland owned by whites who lived in Malakoff. The land was productive, though, and the skills of Presley's father made it even more so. They managed not only to pay their share as rent, but to raise an excess beyond it that let them build up some savings and to buy land of their own.

When Presley came to manhood, his father handed him a working farm, and the young man took it from there. He married, had children, and donated land for a new school. His own children learned to read and write, and one of his grandchildren enrolled in the first class at Jarvis Christian College, established for Blacks in nearby Hawkins in 1912.

Through it all, Presley kept a smile on his face. When he died in 1938, he was mourned by Blacks and whites alike. Sometimes, Liberty works best with a smiling face, a prudent heart, and a bit of good luck.

Anna Thibodeaux

Anna Thibodeaux lived a middle-class Black life in New Orleans in the decades after liberation. The date and place of her birth never made it into an official record. She guessed she'd been born around 1860 and only remembered living in New Orleans.

She raised her children, then her children's children, in the city. As an old woman, she had the joy of holding some of her great-grandchildren as well.

Electricity, moving pictures, and cars fascinated her as she advanced in years, as did the transformations of the city she'd known since childhood.

Her second son, an engineer from Tuskegee, helped build the sanitation infrastructure that tamed cholera and yellow fever in 20th Century Louisiana.

Samuel Langhorne Clemens

Samuel Langhorne Clemens was born in 1835 in Florida, Missouri.

As a young man, he served as a river pilot on the Mississippi River. He moved west thereafter, and his breakthrough as a writer came with his story, "The Celebrated Jumping Frog of Calaveras County," in 1865.

As *Life on the Mississippi*, his recounting of riverboat life, makes clear, the Civil War had a devastating impact on his fellow river pilots.

He rose to fame under the name of **Mark Twain**, and was the leading

American humorist and commentator of the postwar era. Clemens reached his journey's end in Connecticut in 1910.

His posthumous novel, *The War Prayer*, punctured with bitter satire the war fever that had swept the country twice during his lifetime: during the Civil War and in the lead up to the war with Spain. His warning, though pungent, was suppressed during the violent century that followed.

Sometimes, Liberty's heroes get our attention with humor.

Solange Thierry

Solange Thierry came into Liberty's shuffle in the waning days of slavery in southern Louisiana. Her 16-year-old mother was enslaved and her 49-year-old father was her 'owner's' brother. Solange's mother came into the world in a similar manner, born of an enslaved young woman and Solange's great-uncle.

Despite three of her four grandparents being white, Solange had no such status under the perverse racial laws of the time. Her former master and blood relatives did nothing to maintain the ties when liberation came. Solange's mother took her and fled to New Orleans. Her mother died of yellow fever a few years later.

Solange, who despite having light skin and light brown hair, could not be white, was looked upon with suspicion by many in the Black community as well. After living by her wits on her own in New Orleans for several years, she eventually found a way to disappear into a Creole community where many questions were left unasked.

Paul Laurence Dunbar

Paul Laurence Dunbar was born in 1872 in Dayton, Ohio, to parents who had escaped slavery in Kentucky during the Civil War. Paul's father enlisted in the Union Army after his escape, serving in one of the first Black units organized for the conflict.

The younger Dunbar was the first Black student enrolled in Dayton High School, where he counted among his classmates and friends Wilbur and Orville Wright. His classmates and teachers encouraged his literary efforts, and his record of publications began during his young life in Dayton.

His poetry came to the attention of the editors of *Harper's Weekly*, who gave him a larger audience. Dunbar lived a peripatetic existence for many years, wandering the country giving readings and traveling as far as England in his literary efforts.

He settled in Washington, D. C., for a while, where he married and enrolled at Howard University, the "Black Harvard." While there, he was diagnosed with tuberculosis and encouraged to both drink whiskey as a treatment and move west for cleaner air. After a sojourn in Colorado, he returned to Dayton, Ohio.

Despite his literary acclaim, Dunbar had difficulty supporting himself and his mother through writing. His condition worsened in Dayton, and Paul Laurence Dunbar died at age 33 in 1905. Though shortened by illness, his life touched on places and accomplishments that would have been inconceivable before liberation.

Wanada Parker Page

Wanada Parker Page came into the world in 1882 in what was then Indian Territory, now the State of Oklahoma. Her father was Quanah Parker, the last Comanche chief to lead a war against white encroachment on Comanche lands. It was unsuccessful, and the remaining Comanche bands settled onto the reservation where Wanada was born.

Page's grandmother, Quanah Parker's mother, was Cynthia Ann Parker, who had been kidnapped during a Comanche massacre at Fort Parker, Texas, in 1836. Wedded to Chief Peta Nocona thereafter, Cynthia Ann gave birth to Quanah Parker in 1841 at age 14.

Wanada, like her siblings, was taken from her home by the US government and sent to federally run schools designed to assimilate them into the larger culture. She spent the first few years at the Chiloco Indian School, relatively close to home in Oklahoma, but was then sent to the Carlisle Indian School in far-off Pennsylvania in 1894.

She returned to Oklahoma in 1903, marrying a Comanche man named Walter in 1908. He died of tuberculosis in 1912. She worked as an assistant school matron at the Fort Sill Indian School, then studied for and became a nurse's aide, working at the Fort Sill Indian Hospital.

While there, she met and married Harrison Page, a white soldier assigned to the hospital's medical staff. They remained together until Wanada's death in 1970.

Ms. Page was a Christian, a charter member of the Comanche Reformed Church in Lawton, Oklahoma. In her later life, she worked to preserve the memory of her father and grandmother, and to build community between the Indian Parkers in Oklahoma and their white family in Texas.

George Washington Cavin

George Washington Cavin was born in 1855 in Springfield, Missouri. The Cavins were driven from their homes by the violence and terror that scarred Missouri during the Civil War and made their way to Texas. George married his first wife, Victoria Carter, in 1877 in Nacogdoches, Texas.

Cavin helped pioneer the commercial timber industry in East Texas during the postwar years. He established the town of Nivac (his surname, spelled backward) as a timber camp and moved his sawmill elsewhere as the forests around it thinned. In the process, he bought significant acreage north of Nacogdoches.

After the death of his first wife, Cavin married Mary Susan Fraley in 1890, also in Nacogdoches. Between his two marriages, Cavin fathered seven daughters who survived to adulthood. He died in 1937 in the city of Jasper in far southeast Texas, a hundred miles inland from the Gulf of Mexico.

Cavin's descendants continue to gather annually to renew their family bonds. George Cavin represents the first post-Civil War generation rebuilding their lives and country in a transformed region.

May Edward Chinn

May Edward Chinn joined the dance of Liberty in 1896 in Massachusetts. Her father, born in 1852, had escaped slavery at age 11. Her mother, of mixed Native American and African American heritage, was born in 1876.

May's mother saved diligently to send her to boarding school as a child, yet May became ill and had to come home. This worked out better for her, in retrospect. The Tiffany family, for whom May's mother worked, saw to it that the child learned music and languages in their home.

May was unable to finish high school due to poverty, yet she signed up for and passed the entrance test to Columbia Teachers College notwithstanding. She intended to study music, but a negative encounter with a music professor and an excellent beginning in a hygiene class shifted her focus to science.

She completed her degree, then became the first Black woman to enroll in Bellevue College Medical Hospital. She graduated in 1926, but was frozen out of residencies in much of New York because of her race. Harlem Hospital relented and allowed her a residency, but would not give her admitting privileges for many years.

Despite the obstacles, she persevered. She opened a private office and saw patients in their own homes. The latter experience led her to realize the importance of public health measures. She became a vocal advocate.

Her career progressed, and in 1944 she was hired by a New York clinic to lead its cancer research. Dr. Chinn remained there until retirement twenty-nine years later. She retained a lifelong love of music, and was a passionate advocate for Black women in the sciences.

Chinn died in 1980. By virtue of her talent, patience, and persistence, she smashed barriers in her lifetime to pave a wider path for those who came after. Sometimes, Liberty must overcome ridiculous obstacles to express itself.

Louis Armstrong

Louis Armstrong was born in poverty in New Orleans in 1901. His musical skills manifested early in life, yet the path was rocky. When he was 7, the Karnoffskys, a family of Lithuanian Jews, took him under their wing. They were junk dealers and began paying the child to do odd jobs for them.

Two life-shaping developments resulted. First, Mr. Karnoffsky gave the child enough money to buy a cornet from a local pawn shop, putting him on the road to real musicianship. Second, Armstrong saw the ill-treatment the Karnoffskys suffered because of their Jewishness at the hands of other whites. "I was only seven years old," Armstrong wrote later in life, "but I could easily see the ungodly treatment that the white folks were handing the poor Jewish family whom I worked for."

Armstrong's first live performance was at the side of the Karnoffskys' junk wagon, trying to attract customers. Armstrong reportedly wore a Star of David around his neck for the rest of his life in gratitude for their kindness, and sang to his own children the Jewish songs he had learned in childhood.

In 1913, his pre-teen delinquency led to him being sent to the so-named "Colored Waifs Home." The home provided him an opportunity to master an instrument, and the jazz scene in New Orleans at the time exposed him to tremendous musicians.

He began playing professionally at age 17 and soon came to the attention of more prominent artists. In 1922, he was invited to Chicago to join a leading band. His wild improvisational skills and jovial persona led to his artistic breakout. By 1929, he had become one of the nation's most famous musicians.

Having made his name in jazz, Armstrong set out to capture a broader market in the 1930s. His crossover spawned a tremendous run of hit songs, records, and ultimately, movies, that cemented his prominence in American show business. Yet the fact that he had crossed over from pure jazz to more commercial sounds did not sit well with jazz purists. His happy, bubbling stage persona became controversial as well, as the Civil Rights movement reshaped American life beginning in the 1950s.

To some of his Black critics, Armstrong's onstage persona played on longstanding, negative stereotypes of African Americans to appeal to white audiences. They noted that despite his prominence, he seldom discussed race in public and avoided controversy. In critical eyes, he seemed to have sold out his jazz credibility for fame and his race for financial success.

Through it all, Louis Armstrong continued to play, sing, and entertain. After a Grammy-winning role on screen in *Hello, Dolly!* in 1965, he toured almost nonstop for the rest of the decade. Armstrong suffered a debilitating stroke in 1969 and died in 1971.

Though he contributed privately to Dr. Martin Luther King's work, he clearly refused to use his "platform," as we now call it, to further support the cause. To some, this tarnished his legacy. Yet was it not his platform, built by his own efforts, to use as he pleased?

Part of the meaning of Liberty is that we can use it however we want, as long as it doesn't harm others. It allows us to judge for ourselves what pursuits are worth our own involvement, and to what extent we invest ourselves in them.

Ernie Dawkins

Ernie Dawkins came into the world in the mid-1880s, the youngest son of a formerly enslaved couple in rural Maryland. Because Maryland did not secede, slavery there did not end until the 13th Amendment became law in December of 1865. His parents remained on the land, sharecropping a tobacco farm with their former 'owners.'

As a child, Ernie found life on a tobacco farm stifling and longed to leave. At age 17, he did exactly that, settling in Baltimore and finding work as a laborer on the Baltimore and Ohio Railroad. He lived in a boarding house not far from the main rail line in the strictly-segregated city, an arrangement satisfactory to him because his work often kept him out of town.

Eventually, Ernie found a wife and moved into a small house in West

Baltimore. They raised a family, sent their children to public schools, and became a part of their local Missionary Baptist Church. His last assignment with the railroad put him in a central roundhouse.

In the roundhouse, Ernie and his co-workers turned around the enormous train engines on equally enormous turntables. His children and grandchildren remembered his huge, calloused hands and enormous forearms, built through a life of labor.

What amazed both Ernie and his aged parents when they came to live with him was that Ernie labored as he did by his own choice, and his earnings, however small, were his alone. For persons born in bondage or immediately descended from them, that very fact was a wonder.

Ernie may have lived what others would have called a normal, quiet life, but he lived it as a free man. It was concrete fruit of the Liberty Tree.

Zora Neale Hurston

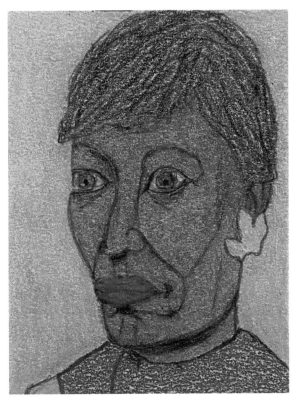

Zora Neale Hurston entered Liberty's dance in Notasulga, Alabama, in 1891, the fifth of eight children born to John and Lucy Potts Hurston. Her father was a carpenter and Baptist preacher, while her mother was a school teacher.

At age 3, her family moved to Eatonville, Florida. Eatonville was one of several all-Black towns organized in the face of the Jim Crow South, where African Americans could live apart from white domination. The place loomed large in her later writing.

She came to Baltimore in her mid-twenties, enrolling at Morgan Academy for a high school course. Formal education was hard to come by for many

Black women in that era, and she was determined to earn her degree. She recorded the year of her birth as 1901, rather than 1891, to qualify for a spot in the public school.

Hurston graduated in 1918, the year World War I ended, and set her sights on Howard University, the "Black Harvard," down the road in Washington, D. C. Hurston's literary life began while she was there.

After attaining her associate's degree at Howard, she was offered a scholarship to Barnard College in New York City, the all-female school twinned to Columbia University, which at the time all-male. She was the only Black woman enrolled. Barnard was her launchpad into the Harlem Renaissance then unfolding.

Hurston's literary output was varied. She wrote news articles, essays, and fiction, and even assisted in writing a play. As her talent became known, she was recruited to write ethnographic accounts of Black life in the South.

Personal life was a struggle. Being a writer wasn't lucrative. She worked for a stretch as a manicurist, freelanced as a journalist, and landed various fellowships. Hurston married three times, each marriage ending in divorce.

Despite her life of publication, she died in poverty in 1960 and was buried in an unmarked grave, her works seemingly forgotten. Beginning in the mid-1970s, though, her writing was rediscovered, and her works found a following in death that had eluded her in life. She produced her most famous novel, *Their Eyes Were Watching God*, in 1937. In 2018, her literary heirs published *Barracoon* from her ethnographic notes about one of the last enslaved persons trafficked into the United States.

Gwendolyn Elizabeth Brooks

Gwendolyn Elizabeth Brooks joined Liberty's story in 1917 in Topeka, Kansas. Her family moved to Chicago when she was a few weeks old, and she spent the rest of her life there.

Her father worked as a janitor to support his family, despite his early aspirations to become a medical doctor. Her mother had been a teacher in Topeka and continued in the profession in Chicago. She was also a concert pianist and a classically-trained musician. Gwendolyn grew up in an atmosphere of intellectual vigor and high culture.

She showed an early interest in writing, which her mother encouraged. "You will be the lady Paul Laurence Dunbar," she told her.

She published her first poem at age 13. After high school, she enrolled in a two-year course at Wilson Junior College and supported herself afterward as a typist. Her ambition, she made clear, was not to be a scholar but a writer.

She wrote to increasing acclaim for the rest of her life. In 1950, Brooks became the first Black woman to win a Pulitzer Prize for Poetry. She was named Poet Laureate of Illinois in 1968, and later served a one-year term as U. S. Poet Laureate.

Brooks died in 2000, one of the fruits of an intellectual Liberty that flowered among the descendants of the freed.

Ralph Ellison

Ralph Ellison was born in 1914, by his own account, in Oklahoma City, Oklahoma. As with many Black families in that era, the Ellisons moved to the North, believing life would be better for their children there. Instead, Ellison's father was killed in a workplace accident, and Ellison's mother, after struggling to find work, returned to Oklahoma.

Ralph finished high school in Oklahoma, taught to play the trumpet by a friend of his father's. He applied to study music at the Tuskegee Institute in

Alabama, that seminal force in Black life in the decades following liberation. They turned him down. A year later, he applied again and was accepted. After hopping freight trains from Oklahoma to Alabama, he enrolled. Like Claude McKay before him, he detested the atmosphere he found there.

Leaving school after three years, Ellison moved to New York City, where a friend encouraged him to write. He did so successfully, and was a part of the Federal Writer's Project from 1938 to 1942. After serving in the Marine Corps during World War II, Ellison returned home and resumed writing.

Ellison spent several years after the war working on a novel, scraping by with occasional literary work and supported by his wife, Fanny. That novel, *The Invisible Man*, came out in 1952 to tremendous success, winning the National Book Award in 1953. Ellison explored in literary form the experience of racism both in the South and the North, his main character being an intelligent, educated man whom others simply did not see because of their preconceptions.

Ellison lived the rest of his life as a literary lion, publishing essays, literary criticism, and short stories, and teaching in various prestigious postings. He never published another novel during his lifetime. After his death in 1994, his literary heirs published a novel in his name from extensive unpublished notes they found among his papers.

Ellison used his Liberty to help illumine the ways in which we see (or do not see) the lives around us.

Cab Calloway

Cabell Calloway III, known to the world as "Cab," made his first appearance in 1907 in Rochester, New York, firmly ensconced in the Black middle-class. Both parents were college graduates. His father was a lawyer, and his mother was a teacher and church musician. In 1919, the family moved from Rochester to Baltimore, Maryland, where Cab's mom had attended college. Cab's father died not long after.

Cab was something of a hustler as a youth, preferring afternoons spent making money to those spent in school. His mother had little patience for it, though. When she caught him shooting dice on the steps of the church where she worked, she sent him to a reform school run by his uncle.

Cab loved jazz, the youth music of the day. His mother and teachers disapproved of it, suspicious of its supposed immorality, but he pursued it anyway. After his high school graduation in 1925, he began performing in nightclubs. His vibrant personality shone brightly on the stage, and he began to make a name for himself.

Cab's mom encouraged him to follow his father's footsteps into practicing law and managed to briefly persuade him to enroll at Crane College in Chicago. The allure of the stage was too strong, though. He dropped out of law school to pursue his music.

Calloway emerged as a distinctive bandleader, composer, and vocalist in the late 1920s and early '30's, the beginning of the swing era. Louis Armstrong taught him "scat" singing, and with his tremendous vocal range and dynamic stage presence, he soared to the heights of American popular music.

Gravitating to New York City, he became a regular at the Cotton Club, a famous musical venue in Harlem at the heart of the Big Band craze. When the house band went out on tour, Calloway was invited to substitute. He formed "Cab Calloway's Cotton Club Orchestra" and ended up sharing house band status for several years with none other than Duke Ellington.

Minnie the Moocher, which Cab wrote and recorded in 1931, became the first recording by a Black artist to sell a million copies. More hits followed, and he branched out into movies. *Stormy Weather*, released in 1943, was the first major Hollywood production with an all-Black cast. His best known late career role came opposite John Belushi and Dan Aykroyd in *The Blues Brothers* in 1980.

He and a friend were arrested and beaten by a Kansas City, Missouri, police officer in 1945 while attempting to visit another friend playing a whites-only club in the city. Both Calloway and his friend ended up in the hospital, accused of being drunk and assaulting the officer.

Calloway's fame drew national attention to the case, though. Several national civil rights groups intervened on his behalf and an investigation followed. As a result, charges were dropped and the cop was fired. Still, the incident illustrated the reality that "Driving While Black" impacted even the highly successful.

He won the National Medal of Arts in 1993 and died in 1994 following a stroke. Cab Calloway persevered throughout his life with immense talent, an irrepressible spirit, and an enduring love of music.

Iosefa Fa'atiu

Iosefa Fa'atiu was born on the island of Tutuila in 1899, the same year a Tripartite Commission in London, on the far side of the globe, divided the Samoan archipelago between Germany and the United States. Tutuila, already home of a major U. S. Naval base, became an American possession.

Iosefa's grandfather was *Matia*, "chief," of his *Aiga*, "extended clan," chosen by the consensus among the family. She grew up helping to keep the family garden, where they grew enough breadfruit, yams, and coconuts to feed themselves year-round. She attended a school founded by Congregational ministers from New England. It was a quiet childhood in what others would have called an idyllic place. Soaring volcanic mountains penetrated lush tropical forests, overlooking the harbor at Pago Pago and the blue Pacific.

World War I in Europe broke out shortly after her fifteenth birthday. The United States was neutral at the start, so the American part of Samoa was not disturbed. Forces from New Zealand landed in the German-run islands in late August, but they took over without firing a shot.

By the time the U. S. entered World War I in 1917, action in the Pacific had long since ceased. Iosefa and the islands escaped the deadliest threat of the war, though: the 1918 influenza epidemic that killed more people worldwide than the conflict itself. Learning from telegraph reports of the disease's spread in Australia and New Zealand, Navy Commander John Martin Poyer isolated the islands, stationing quarantine ships off the coast. Eastern Samoa, under New Zealand governance, suffered the highest rates of infection and death in the Pacific. The American islands were spared.

Iosefa married that same year, and welcomed the first of her seven children in 1919. Life continued for her family in the quiet rhythms of tropical life until the Japanese attack on Pearl Harbor plunged America into World War II. The influx of U. S. Marines into the vital naval base at Pago Pago began almost immediately. Iosefa's three oldest sons were already serving in the local Samoan Marines, which came under direct U. S. command with the war.

In the early morning of January 13, 1942, she awakened to the sound of explosions around the harbor. A Japanese submarine had opened fire on the naval installation. Pago Pago surged to life. American and Samoan Marines sprinted to defensive installations and prepared their weaponry, awaiting an invasion they suspected was imminent.

After fifteen explosions, the shelling stopped. A deadly, fright-filled quiet followed, with the entire island waiting anxiously through the darkness. The day dawned with the Marines still at battle stations, but no invasion fleet loomed offshore. It had been a raid only, and proved to be the only Japanese attack of the war on the islands.

In the aftermath of the raid, though, a patriotic fever swept the islands.

Iosefa's sons were incorporated fully into the U. S. Marines, shipping out for the crunching battles that followed. Her youngest son joined them as soon as he came of age. Miraculously, all four survived.

In the postwar years, all four of her sons left the island permanently for life in the United States. Iosefa remained behind with her daughters and extended family, a U. S. flag proudly flying on her front porch. She died in 1958, having supplied the nation that had claimed her island with the most precious fruit of her garden: her children.

Ralph Mulally

Ralph Mulally came into the world in rural West Virginia in 1910. He spent his working life as a coal miner. It was shift work, with the hours varying from week to week. The schedule became harder as he got older, but coal mining was the only work that paid enough to support a family where he was. He kept working.

On one of his night shift weeks in 1960, he left the mine at dawn, covered head to toe in coal dust. Outside the gate stood U. S. Senator John F. Kennedy. It was 1960, and Kennedy was campaigning for President.

Mulally kept up with the news and knew who Kennedy was. He blurted out, "Senator, the papers say you're a rich man's son."

Kennedy laughed and said, "I suppose that's true."

Mulally thought about it for a moment, then followed up, "Papers say you ain't never done an honest day's work in your life."

Kennedy chuckled again and said, "I suppose that's true, too."

Mulally shook his head and said, "Senator, you ain't missed a damn thing!"

Melvin Reese

Melvin Reese, born in 1911, was the youngest son of agricultural workers in Polk County, Florida. The county at the time was the center of orange cultivation in the United States, and it had a bloody history.

The region had been home to Seminole Indian bands for centuries when the United States acquired Florida from Spain in 1821. The area was placed within the Seminole reservation. The new American overlords regretted the decision, though, and launched a campaign led by future U. S. President Zachary Taylor to remove the indigenous population. It succeeded with brutal efficiency.

Reese's ancestors were brought to the region in the 1850s as enslaved labor on land now owned by whites. When Florida seceded from the Union in 1861, the State government officially organized the county, naming it for a notorious imperialist, former U. S. President James K Polk.

When Reconstruction ended in Florida, Polk County was riven by anti-Black violence, reinforcing the Jim Crow laws that followed the end of Union occupation. Reese's family lived in a tiny rural community a dozen miles south of Bartow, the county seat, stripped of their civil rights and intimidated into compliance. Whites lynched twenty Black men in the county in the two decades surrounding Reese's birth.

The arrival of the phosphate industry in the early 20th Century somewhat eased conditions. With other options available for work, Black workers had a little more Liberty as to where they could sell their labor. Wages rose, though not greatly.

When World War II broke out in 1939, the labor situation changed further. The U. S. government cranked up a military draft in preparation in 1940, reducing further the numbers available for work in the groves. Reese had suffered a workplace accident in his teens and, though he recovered, was rated as 4-F and left undrafted.(According to *Merriam-Webster*, someone classified as "4-F" by a U. S. draft board "is unfit for military service due to physical, mental, or moral reasons.") He and others were well aware of the labor situation.

It came to a head for him when careless white overseers failed to return at the scheduled time to pick him and his crew up from their work in a remote grove. They spent a long, hungry night in the grove, and he protested on behalf of the others. After it happened twice more the next week, he began to organize a strike for better conditions.

He and his family sat bolt upright in their beds in the middle of the night a few days later, awakened by a frantic pounding at their door. A frightened young woman screamed that the Klan was on its way to lynch "uppity Melvin!" He leapt from the house and watched from a nearby thicket.

A dozen men, their identities hidden by sheets, arrived by car and on horseback in front of the house, banging at the door. Not finding him inside, they grabbed his father and dragged him outside. They beat him, stopping short of killing him, then set a makeshift cross ablaze in front of the door and left.

After tending to his father, Reese kissed his parents goodbye and fled on foot. After walking out of the groves, he hopped various freight trains and hitchhiked his way north to Detroit, where he found wartime work in Ford's River Rouge facility.

Melvin Reese never returned to Florida. He eventually prospered enough to bring his elderly parents to live with him.

Joseph Bonanno

Joseph Bonanno, born on the Italian island of Sicily in 1905, was brought at age three by his family to America. The family returned to Sicily ten years later, and his father, a member of the Sicilian mafia, died of a heart attack there in 1915.

At age 19, in 1924, Bonanno reentered the United States as a stowaway on a boat from Cuba. Immigration authorities apprehended him on arrival, but he was soon released as a "favor" to another mobster. He became the youngest-ever boss of a major crime family in 1931.

In 1963, apparently dissatisfied with business arrangements, Bonanno plotted to assassinate several other members of the so-called Crime Commission that the major mafia families had set up to keep the peace. The plot came to light among the others, and he fled to Canada.

He returned to New York in 1964, but disappeared soon after for his own safety. Bonanno resurfaced in 1968 after two years of gang warfare in the family he once led. After suffering a heart attack, he agreed to end the war and retire to Arizona.

In 1983, he published his memoirs, *A Man of Honor: The Autobiography of Joseph Bonanno*. Michael Kora, editor of Bonanno's memoirs, said of him, "In a world where most of the players were, at best, semiliterate, Bonanno read poetry, boasted of his knowledge of the classics, and gave advice to his cohorts in the form of quotes from Thucydides or Machiavelli."

Joseph Bonanno died in 2002 in Arizona, at the age of 97. An illegal immigrant and a violent criminal, Bonanno illustrates the peril to many of Liberty without conscience.

Luis Tiant, Sr.

Luis Tiant, Sr., was born Luis Eleuterio Tiant Bravo on the baseball-mad island of Cuba in 1906. Growing up in Havana, he soon showed exceptional talent on the diamond. Tiant rose through the ranks to the Cuban national team and began pitching professionally in 1926 with his hometown Havana Red Sox. Four seasons of pitching professionally in Cuba and barnstorming with teams in the Caribbean followed, before he joined the Cuban Stars West of the American-based Negro National Leagues.

In 1935, Tiant signed with the New York Cubans, moving to the United States. He remained with them through 1940, then spent the 1941 season pitching for Veracruz Aguila in the Mexican League. American entry into

World War II had a drastic impact on the Negro Leagues, and Tiant seems to have sat out 1942 for lack of opportunity.

He returned to the New York Cubans when the Negro Leagues resumed full play in 1943 and remained with them through 1947. Tiant spent his last pro season pitching for two teams in the Mexican League, retiring at age 41. After each of his professional seasons abroad, he returned to Cuba to pitch winter league ball there.

A three-time Negro League All-Star, Luis Tiant won the Negro League World Series with the New York Cubans in 1947. At the time, Luis was excluded from the American Major Leagues because of his race: only whites were allowed. Since December of 2020, Major League Baseball has included select Negro League statistics of that era with its own.

Tiant and his wife Isabela's only child, Luis Clemente Tiant Vega, was born in 1940 in Havana. The younger Luis idolized his father and wanted to follow in his footsteps, but the elder Tiant discouraged him. There was no money in baseball, he said. Young Luis should study something that will get him a job.

Yet young Luis wouldn't be held back. After a year studying to be an electrician, he gave it up to return to baseball and emerged as a standout pitcher himself. In 1957, young Luis made the Cuban national youth team, attracting the attention of an American scout. On the scout's recommendation, he began pitching in the Mexican League where his father had played.

Meanwhile, the Cuban Revolution brought Fidel Castro to power in 1959. Civil liberties on the island began to erode, and in 1961, the elder Luis advised his son not to return to Cuba when his season abroad ended. He feared young Luis would not be allowed to leave again.

Luis and Isabela waited fourteen long years before they saw him again. In the interim, the younger Luis had risen to stardom in the American Major Leagues.

After a private appeal from an American politician, the elder Tiants were permitted to travel to see their son play. The three reunited before a Boston Red Sox home game on August 26, 1975.

Luis and Isabela remained in Massachusetts with their son, the elder Tiant dying the following year. Luis Eleuterio Tiant Bravo was re-christened "Luis Tiant, Sr." by the American press in 1975, to distinguish him from "Luis Tiant, Jr." his son.

Francis Albert Sinatra

Francis Albert "Frank" Sinatra entered the world in a tenement apartment in Hoboken, New Jersey, in 1915. He nearly didn't make it. He was a huge newborn born to a tiny woman, and the difficult birth left him with permanent injuries to his ear.

His parents, Marty and Dolly Sinatra, were immigrants from Italy. Marty, who never learned to read and write, was a boxer as a young man and spent his working life with the Hoboken Fire Department. Because of his own illiteracy, he urged his son to get the best education he could. Dolly, his mother, was a force of nature: working as a midwife, running a tavern with her husband, and becoming a political organizer in her neighborhood. Frank reflected her iron will and personal charisma.

Young Frank attempted to follow his father's urging. He attended school, being expelled from one a month before graduation for "excessive rowdiness." He worked for a while as a riveter in Hoboken, yet music was in his blood.

He relentlessly worked at improving his singing skills, paying for elocution lessons and using various exercises to enhance his vocal stamina. It began to pay off in 1935 when Frank was hired to sing professionally on a broadcast radio program. In those pre-television days, radio was the medium of everyday life.

Bandleader Harry James heard him on the radio and hired him for his band. Sinatra cut his first records with James. Tommy Dorsey, an even bigger name, hired him away from James, and Sinatra's stratospheric ascent began.

In 1943, Sinatra left Dorsey and went solo. "Sinatramania" ensued: a succession of hit records, raucous appearances, and screaming crowds of "bobbysoxers" wherever he appeared. Frank's hard work and charisma had carried the day.

His first credited film role came the same year. Sinatra turned out to be an outstanding actor, winning an Oscar for his role in *From Here to Eternity* in 1954. He helped pioneer the Las Vegas Strip as an entertainment mecca and reached iconic status in American culture.

His personal life was tumultuous. He was a relentless perfectionist with a hair-trigger temper. Rumors of mob ties followed him, though he always dismissed them. He married four times, the first three ending in divorce. Rated 4-F by his local draft board, he did not serve during World War II. Controversy swirled about what exactly led to his 4-F status. (According to *Merriam-Webster*, someone classified as "4-F" by a U. S. draft "is unfit for military service due to physical, mental, or moral reasons.")

Through all the ups and downs, though, Frank persevered. Nicknamed "Chairman of the Board" and "Ol' Blue Eyes," he led his "Rat Pack" group of close friends from his Vegas hangouts to the end of his life. Sinatra famously advocated for Black artists, boycotting venues that excluded them. Though Catholic, he generously supported Jewish charities through the decades.

After winning eleven Grammys during his career, Sinatra received the Presidential Medal of Freedom in 1985 from his longtime friends, Ronald and Nancy Reagan. Frank Sinatra, the oversized infant who almost didn't see his first day of life, died in 1998 at the age of 82.

Judy Tyler

Judy Tyler was born into a show business family in 1932. Her father was a jazz trumpeter who played with Benny Goodman. Her mother once danced for the famous Ziegfeld Follies in New York.

Judy studied ballet, music, and acting. At 17, she won a beauty contest, and became a star in the new medium of television with a role on *The Howdy Doody Show*. She spent two years on the program, then left to take a role in a Broadway play. The subsequent publicity landed her on the cover of *Life* magazine. At that time, *Life* magazine was a leading light in American culture.

Judy divorced her first husband early in 1957 and remarried a few months later. All the while, her personal star shone brighter and brighter. Her second feature film was *Jailhouse Rock*, starring opposite Elvis Presley in his first movie.

Three days after production wrapped, Judy and her husband set out on the cross country drive back to their home in New York. They swerved to avoid a trailer on the road in Wyoming, and were killed in a head-on collision. She was 24.

According to reports, Elvis was so distraught over her death that he was never able to watch the movie they had starred in together.

George Cunyus

George Cunyus came into this world in Dallas in 1930, a few years after his young parents had been fired from their jobs as teachers in a small, East Texas town. George's dad, a science teacher, insisted on teaching the Theory of Evolution. His employers were not amused.

George grew up in the Oak Cliff section of Dallas and then went to college, graduating in 1951. Thereafter, he was drafted into the U. S. Army in an era when even college boys did their part for the nation. The Korean War was raging in northeast Asia at the time, so after basic training and a whirlwind marriage, he shipped out for the front. He later joked about the "All Expense Paid Tour of Korea" the U. S. Army had given him as a wedding present.

From a hillside in Korea, he applied to law school. Sight unseen, SMU Law

School in Dallas accepted him. The U. S. government paid his tuition under the GI Bill, honoring the promise it made to those who defended Liberty. While George was a law student, he campaigned for class president using the slogan, "Throw the Rascal In!"

Apparently, he did not win.

Despite that, he went on to have a productive career as a lawyer in his hometown.

Benjamin Franklin Kelly

The State of Texas vigorously upheld its "color line," formal racial segregation, as long as possible, excluding not just its Black population from full participation in society but its Latino population as well. Practically nowhere else was it so fiercely maintained as among its major college football teams. The University of Texas fielded the last all-white national championship team in 1969, going 10-0 and defeating Notre Dame in the Cotton Bowl.

Cracks had appeared in the wall before that. Hayden Fry at SMU recruited Jerry Levias out of Beaumont, Texas, in 1965 as the first Black scholarship player in the Texas-dominated Southwest Conference. Despite facing racial abuse on and off the field, Levias rewarded SMU with three straight all-conference selections, an SWC title, and All-American honors in 1968. The other conference schools grudgingly began recruiting Black athletes to remain competitive.

Before Jerry Levias, though, there was Benjamin Franklin "Ben" Kelly. Born in 1931 in San Angelo, Texas, Kelly starred at his segregated high school and earned a football scholarship to the University of Illinois. The Korean War intervened, though, and Kelly served his country for two years.

He returned to San Angelo in 1953 after the Army, still eager to play. He approached the coaches at Angelo College, a two-year institution in town that later became Angelo State University. The coaches took him directly to college president, Rex Johnston. Johnston interviewed Kelly, then personally led him to the registrar's office to enroll.

The task wasn't finished until Johnston went to the college's Board of Trustees and specifically asked permission for Kelly to play. They agreed, and Kelly crossed the color line in Texas college football in the fall of 1953. He did so with much success, starting on offense and defense for two years and earning all-conference honors.

After spending a year playing professionally with the Los Angeles Rams, he returned to San Angelo and spent his life working with children and youth through the local Boys and Girls Club. Ben Kelly cracked the wall of segregation in Texas sports, aided by Rex Johnston and a forward-looking Board of Trustees. Many others followed, and Texas itself is much better for it.

Mary Ellen Faust

Mary Ellen Faust was born in Decatur, Illinois, in 1932, though she laid no claim to it as a birthplace and was slightly embarrassed by the "Yankee" association all her days. Her parents were both from the hills of western Arkansas. Her father, J. J., an irascible medical graduate with a brilliant mind, happened to be finishing his residency in radiology at the time in Decatur.

The son of an itinerant Methodist preacher, J. J. arrived in Waldron, Arkansas, as a teen, near the end of his father's career. The family of her mother, Ellen, had been in Waldron for a couple of generations by then. Ellen had been dating the pharmacist's son until J. J. came along. Seeing in him someone with the drive and intelligence to get her out of small-town western Arkansas, she gladly switched allegiances and held on tight. Only decades later did she admit what so motivated her to leave: she had been abused as a teen by a pastor in her local church.

After Mary Ellen's birth, J. J. completed his residency, and the family moved to Tyler, Texas, then a small town in the piney woods. The town was building a new hospital, though, and J. J. was its first radiologist. His work provided the means, and Ellen provided the drive, with the result that Mary Ellen grew up in the strictly segregated, high-society world of Rose Parades and debutantes. She recalled later that Tyler had two high schools when she was there: Tyler White, and Tyler Black.

Like her mother a generation before, she too was eager to leave the place where she grew up. She graduated early from high school, spent two years at Tyler Junior College, and then enrolled at Southern Methodist University in Dallas, ninety miles to the west.

True to the high society female ethos of her era, she joked later about the two degrees she earned in Dallas: her B. A. from SMU, and her Mrs. from her husband. Mary Ellen gave birth to three sons, and was an artistic, energetic presence in the world around her.

Tragically, her exposure to X-rays as the child of a doctor exploring a new field caused lasting harm to her health. She battled cancer twice and won. The third time, though, there was no escaping, and she died, age 55, in Dallas.

Joe Cornelius

Joseph Burgess Cornelius, Sr., came into the world in the town of Minden, Louisiana, in 1942. Minden is a small city of roughly 11,000, located in north-central Louisiana thirty miles east of Shreveport. He spent the majority of his life there, graduating from the segregation-era Webster High School in town.

He tried his hand briefly in New York City, and was a funeral home technician for a while in Shreveport, but Minden was where he invested his efforts. He served there as a sheriff's deputy. He also owned and operated an ice cream truck, to the delight of the town's children.

Cornelius and his wife, Jacquelyn, raised four children, three of whom survived him. He once was the head of the Minden High School Booster Club, participated annually in the Martin Luther King, Jr., Day and Black History Month observances, and was active in city government. One of his passions was raising funds to send young people to summer camps nearby.

Joe Cornelius ran for and won a City Council seat in 1991. He lost his reelection bid in 1995, but remained involved, advocating for better services in Minden's Black neighborhoods. He ran again and won in 2010. Named Mayor Pro Tem by the Council, he became Mayor in 2013 upon the death of a long-serving office holder. Cornelius ran to complete the mayoral term, but was defeated. He remained on the City Council.

On September 1, 2024, Cornelius and his daughter Keisha were shot to death by Keisha's 11-year-old son, Cornelius's grandson. Though various theories have been put forward as to the child's motives, one fact is undeniable: the boy had easy access to a loaded firearm, whatever his grievance may have been.

Bob Newhart

Bob Newhart came into the world in 1929 in Oak Park, Illinois, a western suburb of Chicago. Newhart began his working life as an accountant, whose humor often left his co-workers convulsed with laughter. He took his talents onto the stand-up comedy stage in the late 1950s, where his deadpan, stammering style quickly gained a wide following.

The former accountant first appeared on television on *Playboy's Penthouse* in 1959. A year later, a comedy album he recorded live at the Tidelands Motel in Houston reached #1 on Billboard's comedy charts, and he attained an unlikely nationwide fame. In a sense, Newhart was postwar America's comic "Everyman."

Newhart's comedic career spanned parts of seven decades. He played the lead in two smash-hit television series, made hundreds of appearances as himself on variety shows, and starred in movies including the hit *Elf*, with Will Ferrell and James Caan. He won his only Primetime Emmy for his late-career role in *The Big Bang Theory*.

Beneath the veneer of stardom, though, he remained the same soft-spoken, modest, and thoughtful human being he'd been before fame took hold. Newhart married once, to Ginny, in 1963. They raised four children and remained together until Newhart's death in 2024.

Shelley Duvall

Shelley Alexis Duvall was born in 1949 in Fort Worth, Texas, a place where her parents never planned to deliver their child. Her mother happened to be in town visiting her own mother when she went into labor with Shelley. The family returned to Houston, baby in tow, after her birth.

Though interested in the arts, Duvall never set out to be an actor. She was working as a cosmetics saleswoman in 1970 when scouts for director Robert Altman discovered her at a party. Altman persuaded her to take a role in the movie *Brewster McCloud* in 1970.

Impressed by her quirky screen presence, Altman cast her in subsequent films as well and she became an unlikely star. Perhaps her most memorable role came opposite Jack Nicholson in Stanley Kubrick's adaptation of Stephen King's novel, *The Shining*. Kubrick was a notorious perfectionist.

Of the multiple takes Kubrick required to shoot scenes, Duvall later said, "Have you seen the film *Groundhog Day*? Well, that's what it was like."

Duvall appeared in 55 different roles between 1970 and apparent retirement in 2002. She came out of retirement for one further appearance in 2023. Duvall married only once, in 1970, and the marriage ended in divorce in 1974. She died in Texas at the age of 75 in 2024.

Elsie Flowers

Elsie Flowers, born in the war year of 1944 in Montgomery, Alabama, never thought of herself as anything other than an ordinary woman doing ordinary things in the world. She grew up, finished high school, found a job at the U. S. Postal Service, and got married. She and husband Bruce raised four children in the Black middle-class in Alabama's capital.

Yet she had a front-row seat to historic developments. Flowers came of age as the Civil Rights Movement was reaching a crescendo, with Montgomery at its heart. Fully enfranchised as a result of it, she played an attentive, if small-scale, role in her community's political life, almost entirely through the life of Hutchinson Missionary Baptist Church, where she attended.

Her husband died of a heart attack at the young age of 37, and Elsie was left to finish raising the children. This she did as well, opening her home at the same time to other children around her whose families were struggling. Her home became a mecca of sanity because of her gentle, abiding presence at its heart.

In the 1990s, Elsie's daughter returned home after losing her own husband, and the house again filled with the activities of children. This time, the pressing issue in the neighborhoods around her was the crack epidemic, rather than civil rights. Elsie tuned in to it with fierce attention, fearing intensely for her grandchildren and watching the terrible toll it took on others around them.

Yet she did so in her characteristic gentle, jovial way. Her home remained a mecca of sanity, and somehow, some way, she and her daughter managed to raise young people who resisted the worst impulses around them. Through it all, she was the rock holding her family to the "straight and narrow" in an era of great urban upheaval.

When she died in 2013, mourners at her funeral recognized her as the unsung hero she was. She never attained wealth or fame. The larger world knew nothing of her. Yet she raised thriving children and grandchildren despite the odds.

The mourners also remembered the signature applesauce cake she baked for church suppers and special family occasions. It was, they said, to die for.

Tsung-Dao Lee

Tsung-Dao Lee came into the world in Shanghai, China, in 1926. China had been in turmoil for the previous thirty years. Foreign plunderers had intruded into its very heart. The major world powers had carved out exclusive zones along its coast by the use of force and unequal treaties. Its ancient imperial government was overthrown by revolution in 1911, and Japan, looming across the Yellow Sea, set its sights on building an empire at China's expense.

Lee, the third of six children, grew up in a "family of learning" in the great

Chinese port. The Japanese invasion in 1937 interrupted his formal schooling and forced the family into internal exile. His brilliance manifested itself despite his lack of a formal education, and he was admitted in 1943 to National Chekiang University, then located in its own internal exile in Guizhou. Though Lee intended to study chemical engineering, his professors recognized his gifts and persuaded him to study physics.

The war continued. and in 1945 he relocated to National Southwestern Associated University in Kunming. Lee, with only two years of college, received a fellowship from the Chinese government in 1946 and began doctoral studies at the University of Chicago in the United States. By the time he finished his Ph.D. in 1950, the Chinese Communist Party had defeated the Nationalists and taken over the country.

Lee remained in the United States. Appointed an Assistant Professor of Physics at Columbia University at age 29, Lee did groundbreaking work with a colleague. He became the first person of Chinese origin to win a Nobel Prize in 1957, at the age of 31.

Though he became a U. S. citizen in 1962, Lee never lost his love for the land of his birth. When relations between China and the U. S. finally thawed in the late 1970s, he was able to resume contacts and return home to visit. He established and maintained a close working relationship from his home in America with the Tsung-Dao Lee Institute at the Jiao Tong University, named for him in his hometown of Shanghai.

Lee died in 2024, his life spent expanding the frontiers of learning in physics and rebuilding scientific relationships between his homeland and his adopted country.

Luis Tiant, Jr.

Luis Tiant, Jr., like his father, was a Cuban-born baseball standout. During the late 1950s, he rose to stardom on Cuba's national team. He continued pitching for the national team after the Cuban revolution that brought Fidel Castro to power.

In 1961, while Luis was pitching at a tournament in Mexico, his father advised him that if he returned to Cuba, he wouldn't be allowed to leave again. Tiant stayed in Mexico, ultimately signed with the Boston Red Sox, and became a Major League Baseball All-Star pitcher. He was beloved by Red Sox fans, who often chanted, "*El Tiante!*" when he pitched.

His parents were not permitted to travel from Cuba, and Luis, Jr., did not see them at all for fourteen years. After Tiant became an All-Star, a prominent American politian appealed privately to Castro to allow the senior Tiants to travel to see their son pitch. Castro agreed, and the Tiant family was reunited in Boston in 1975.

Luis Tiant, Jr., died in 2024. Through his talent and his father's foresight, Tiant retained his Liberty. Through his baseball stardom and two sympathetic politicians, he obtained Liberty for his parents as well.

George H W Bush

George Herbert Walker Bush was born into a well-to-do family in Massachusetts in 1924. His father, Prescott Bush, relocated them to Connecticut during George's childhood. The elder Bush subsequently ran for and won a US Senate seat in his adopted State.

Educated at the elite Phillips Academy in Massachusetts, Bush postponed higher education to volunteer for the U. S. Navy during World War II. He was commissioned as an ensign in 1943, one of the youngest officers to serve during the war. Assigned to the Pacific Theater, Bush was shot down during a bombing run over Chichijima in 1944. He bailed out over the open sea, the only one of the three in his aircrew to survive. USS Finback plucked him from the ocean.

He married his fiancée, Barbara, while home on leave in early 1945. After finishing a degree at Yale University, Bush moved his family to Midland, Texas, building a successful oil company in the postwar period.

Once established in the oil business, he moved to Houston and became involved in politics. The Democratic Party had long dominated Texas, and Bush in the mid-1960s played a key part in a Republican resurgence there. Along the way, he served as a Congressman from Texas, Ambassador to the United Nations, Chairman of the Republican National Committee, Chief of Liaison to the People's Republic of China, and Director of the CIA.

He ran for president in 1980, losing the nomination to Ronald Reagan. Reagan tapped him to be his vice presidential candidate, and the two were elected in 1980. Bush served eight years as Vice President. then won a term as President in 1988 on Reagan's retirement.

Bush's presidency had moments of profound triumph. He oversaw the end of the Cold War and the reunification of Germany. He watched carefully the collapse of the Soviet Union, America's Cold War adversary, and gathered the coalition that reversed Iraq's invasion of Kuwait.

His stratospheric popularity at the end of the first Gulf War didn't last. The economy tanked toward the end of his term. Critics pilloried him for breaking his repeated campaign pledge: "Read my lips. No new taxes." However unpopular his willingness to compromise may have made him, the deal he struck with Congress set the stage for a federal fiscal resurgence in the 1990s.

Bill Clinton defeated his reelection bid in 1992, and Bush retired into private life. He and Clinton famously became dear friends after Clinton left office, often working together on important humanitarian issues.

George H. W. Bush died in his adopted hometown of Houston in 2018. According to one of his sons, "He looked for the good in each person, and he usually found it."

Nancy Pelosi

Nancy D'Alessandro Pelosi, born in 1940 in Baltimore, Maryland, is the daughter of Thomas and Annunciata D'Allesandro. Her mother immigrated to the United States from Italy in 1912. Nancy's father was a U. S. Congressman when she was born and later served as Mayor of Baltimore. Nancy has been a lifelong, practicing Catholic, though not without controversy from other Catholics for her pro-choice views.

After finishing a Catholic education, she married Paul Pelosi in 1963 and moved to the Bay Area of California. She inherited considerable political skill from her father and became a force in the California Democratic Party, all while raising her five children. She was elected Chair of the California Party in 1981.

First elected to the U. S. House of Representatives in 1987, she immediately worked to improve treatment and care for persons stricken by the AIDS epidemic then raging. She campaigned against handgun violence and became a tireless advocate for health care reform. In the run-up to the

U. S. invasion of Iraq, Pelosi was one of the few prominent Democrats to vote against its authorization. Because of her effectiveness within the halls of power, she also became a lightning rod for Republican opposition.

As the years passed, her effectiveness only increased. She became the first woman to lead a Congressional political caucus in either major party in 2003. As Party leader, she became the first woman to serve as Speaker of the House in 2007. She reverted to Minority Leader when the House passed into Republican hands in 2011, and rose again to the speakership in 2019.

Renowned for her toughness and political skill, she scotched an effort by House Democrats to impeach President George W. Bush in 2007. During her second stint as speaker, she successfully led two efforts to impeach President Donald Trump. The first effort grew out of a controversial phone conversation between Trump and Ukrainian President Volodymyr Zelenskyy, in which Trump appeared to use a hold on U. S. aid to force Zelenskyy into a partisan investigation of a Trump opponent.

The second successful impeachment followed a riot at the U. S. Capitol on January 6, 2021, in which an enraged mob of Trump supporters stormed the building and interrupted the certification of electoral votes from the 2020 election. Trump had lost the election, but claimed otherwise. Pelosi personally was a target of the mob, as was then-Vice President Mike Pence.

Both motions to impeach passed the House under Pelosi's leadership, and both failed to reach the required 2/3rds majority needed in the Senate to convict, remove, and, in the second case, bar Trump from future office.

In 2022, another enraged Trump supporter broke into Pelosi's San Francisco home. She was not home. The man instead assaulted Paul Pelosi with a hammer. The assailant was arrested, tried, convicted, and imprisoned. Mr. Pelosi, already an elderly man when attacked, has had a difficult recovery from his injuries.

After twenty years leading her Party in the House and eight years as Speaker, Pelosi stepped back from her leadership position in 2023. She remained in office, still wielding enormous influence built over a lifetime of work. She remains a lightning rod for the opposition, continuing to draw the angry denunciations of her opponents even after giving up her leadership position.

Pelosi, daughter of an immigrant, has had a barrier-shattering life and career in politics. Like her or not, she has presented a master class throughout her political life in how to succeed in the American political process.

Rupert Murdoch

Rupert Murdoch was born in Melbourne, Australia, in 1931, son of a famous Australian World War I correspondent who had gone into publishing after the war. Rupert was a bright young man. He went away to far-off England to study at Oxford University, and afterwards briefly worked as an editor in an English news organization.

At his father's death, Murdoch returned to Australia and took over the two newspapers his father owned. Under his leadership, the papers burst free of their strait-laced ethos, adopting tabloid-style headlines and story-telling. Circulation soared, profits rolled in, and young Rupert began acquiring other media outlets in his homeland.

Not content to dominate the news business in Australia, he began buying up news properties in England as well. He kept to the sensational style that had proven profitable at home, and soon enjoyed similar success in the United Kingdom. He also presented a consistently conservative voice through the editorial pages, something of an anomaly in a business that had predominantly leaned left before.

As his success built, Murdoch cast his eye on the biggest market among the English-speaking nations: the United States. Here, entry into the market was severely limited by American restrictions on foreign ownership. He moved to the United States permanently in 1974 to begin addressing the issue.

In 1985, he became a naturalized U. S. citizen. The restrictions gone, he bought *Twentieth Century-Fox* that year and began accumulating other television and media properties. Three major TV networks dominated American airwaves in those days: ABC, NBC, and CBS. Under Murdoch's leadership, the Fox network emerged as their rival. He scored a major coup in 1993, striking a deal with the most popular American sports league, the NFL, to broadcast its games.

Murdoch's network and his Fox News cable network rapidly grew in influence. By the end of the 1990s, Fox News had eclipsed cable news pioneer CNN to become the highest-rated outlet in the segment. This gave Murdoch and his network unprecedented influence in American politics in general, and conservative politics in particular.

Having built an American broadcast juggernaut, he set out to do the same in the United Kingdom. His Sky News network there soon paralleled its U.S. counterpart in influence. As his networks grew, of course, so did scrutiny of them and of him in political circles in both countries.

Murdoch, so successful in building a media behemoth, led a troubled personal life. He married five times, four of those marriages ending in divorce. He has fathered six children. As of this writing, succession plans at his media empire remain muddled.

Through it all, Murdoch has skillfully used his Liberty to expand his brand

and give voice to positions he felt were overlooked, exerting tremendous influence on political processes throughout the English-speaking world as he did so. Whether that influence has been for the better or not depends on one's perspective.

Rudolph Giuliani

Rudolph Giuliani was born in Brooklyn, New York in 1944, the grandson of Italian immigrants. Raised in a devoted Catholic family, he considered becoming a priest before deciding to practice law instead. Giuliani made his reputation as a crusading prosecutor, campaigning against the Mafia. He had significant success doing so, and began to set his sights on a political career.

He first ran for Mayor of New York in 1989, losing narrowly to David Dinkins. Four years later, still building on his image as a guardian of law and order, he ran again and won. For several years, he presided over the city as crime rates fell and the once-beleaguered community seemed to revitalize. He was re-elected in 1997.

Though term-limited and unable to run again for Mayor, Mr. Giuliani was still in office on September 11, 2001. Ironically, primary elections to find his successor were scheduled that very day. Instead, al-Qaeda extremists launched the most successful terrorist attack in American history. The world watched in horror as the Twin Towers of New York's World Trade Center were struck by hijacked airliners and later collapsed.

Mr. Giuliani's firm leadership reassured a frightened public in the aftermath of the attack. He told New Yorkers and the world, "Tomorrow New York is going to be here. And we're going to rebuild, and we're going to be stronger than we were before ... I want the people of New York to be an example to the rest of the country, and the rest of the world, that terrorism can't stop us."

For several years thereafter, he was known as "America's Mayor." Despite his fame, he failed in his campaign for U. S. President in 2008, losing the Republican nomination to John McCain. He continued his work in the law, thereafter, ultimately being appointed by President Donald Trump as Trump's personal lawyer. Giuliani's efforts on Trump's behalf after the latter's loss to Joe Biden in the 2020 presidential election were not successful. The ensuing controversies have been kind neither to his livelihood nor his reputation.

Joseph R. Biden, Jr.

Joseph Robinette "Joe" Biden, Jr., was born in Scranton, Pennsylvania, in 1942, raised there and in Delaware, where his family moved in 1953. An honor graduate at the University of Delaware, he went on to earn a law degree at Syracuse University.

Coming home to Delaware after law school, he immediately became involved in politics. After two years on the Newcastle County council, he scored an upset win in 1972 in a campaign for the U. S. Senate. Only 29 at the time, he was the fifth youngest U. S. Senator in history.

Yet Biden's storybook rise took an immediate and tragic turn. A month after his election and before taking office, his wife Neilia and their three children were in a serious auto accident. Neilia and her infant daughter were killed. Biden's two young sons, Beau and Hunter, were seriously injured.

He seriously considered giving up his political career, but was persuaded not to by friends. Biden became a fixture thereafter on the Amtrak train between Washington, D.C., and his Delaware home, commuting home each night after the Senate session to be with his boys. In 1977, he remarried, and he went on to win reelection to the Senate six times.

His family life back on track with his second wife, Jill, Biden had higher ambitions. He ran for president the first time in 1988, his campaign undone by accusations that he had plagiarized speeches by a British politician. He ran a second time in 2008. After failing to make an impact, he withdrew from a race that Illinois Senator Barack Obama eventually won. Obama tapped him as his Vice Presidential candidate, though, and he joined the campaign. Obama and Biden won twice, and Joe served eight years as Vice President.

During his Vice Presidential term, his son Beau, an Iraq War veteran and a rising star in Delaware politics, died of brain cancer. His younger son Hunter struggled through significant issues with addiction. In the midst of it, Vice President Biden was passed over as Obama's heir in 2016 in favor of Hillary Clinton.

Mrs. Clinton lost her race unexpectedly to Republican candidate Donald Trump. Four years later, Biden ran for and won the Democratic nomination, then defeated Trump in the general election. He received the most votes ever in a U. S. presidential election up to that date. At the time, he was the oldest person ever to hold the presidency.

Biden came into office against the backdrop of a raging COVID epidemic, and a first-ever effort by a losing President to remain in office. He served his term and locked up renomination in 2024 without significant intra-party competition. However, a disastrous performance in a televised debate with Trump triggered widespread panic among Democrats about his age and prospects for reelection.

After intense pressure, he dropped out of the race in favor of his Vice President, Kamala Harris, hoping she could hold on to the office. She couldn't, as Trump reclaimed the presidency and his party scored a resounding victory.

Donald Trump

Donald Trump is the fourth of five children born to Fred and Mary Trump of Queens, New York. Fred's parents were German immigrants. Mary herself was an immigrant from Scotland. Mr. Trump was born in 1946, the very first year of the so-called "Baby Boom."

Mr. Trump's father and grandfather had outstanding business skills. Fred Trump, Donald's father, had amassed a significant real estate portfolio by the time his son came into the business in the early 1970s. The younger Trump turned that foundation into a global brand, spinning off into a highly successful television series, *The Apprentice*, which ran from 2004 to 2015.

Mr. Trump took his polarizing brand and his idiosyncratic genius as a communicator into American politics, running for and winning the U. S. Presidency in 2016. He lost his reelection bid in 2020 to Joe Biden, though Trump protested vigorously that the election had been stolen from him.

In 2024, he again ran for President, becoming the first person since Franklin D Roosevelt to win a major party's presidential nomination three consecutive times. A bitterly contested general election campaign followed, in which he survived two assassination attempts. Three months before the election, after a calamitous debate, the Democrats dumped their candidate, sitting President Joe Biden, in favor of Vice President Kamala Harris.

Trump and his party won a surprisingly solid victory. In doing so, he became the first person since Grover Cleveland in the 1890s to win non-consecutive terms as president.

Bill Gates

William Henry Gates III, "Bill," was born in Seattle, Washington, in 1955. Precociously brilliant and focused on computers in that pre-personal computer era, he entered Harvard for college but stayed only two years. His skills were already too much in demand for further formal education. No college course taught what Gates was learning to do on his own at the time.

As the computing revolution gathered steam in the 1970s, American-based IBM took a dominating lead in the race to build hardware. They paid relatively little attention to the operating software that brought the hardware to life. Gates, on the other hand, made that his focus together with his childhood friend and business partner Paul Allen. Gates and his startup, Microsoft, signed a contract in November, 1980, to supply IBM's operating software.

The revolution followed. As IBM licensed other companies to build computers along similar lines, Microsoft stepped up to provide software for them. "Big Blue," as IBM was known, and its licensees soon swept other personal computing platforms aside. IBM realized too late that it had focused on the wrong end of the revolution. Hardware was interchangeable: software was the key.

Gates and Microsoft surged to a dominant position in the radical transformation smaller-scale computing brought first to the American and then to the global economy. By the middle of the 1980s, Microsoft was one of the biggest companies in the world, and Gates one of the world's richest men. At its peak in the 1990s, Gates and Microsoft held 90% of the global market for software operating systems. Its moves into office software and the fledgling internet only boosted its market power. Gates became for his era to what John D Rockefeller had been for his.

As with Rockefeller, Gates's success drew the attention and ire of bypassed competitors and of the U. S. government. A series of antitrust actions against Microsoft's monopolistic practices followed, eventually forcing the company to cease bundling its various products so tightly together as to make competition unlikely. The dynamic nature of the computer industry also tended to make the monopoly unstable. Still, Microsoft evolved and continued to thrive.

Gates married Melinda French in 1994, and the couple had three children. Gates often stated his intention to give away the vast majority of his fortune, rather than leave it entirely to his heirs. He and wife Melinda formed the Bill and Melinda French Gates Foundation in 2000 to do exactly that. The Gates divorced in 2021.

Bill Gates, like Rockefeller before him, turned his attention to philanthropy in the middle of his working life. Like Rockefeller, he focused on scientifically solid, real-world results in combating global poverty and endemic disease. Also like Rockefeller, his philanthropic work has had and continues to have a profound impact on the world.

Gates, again like Rockefeller before him, has become a lightning rod for critics of his wealth and enduring influence. Various conspiracy theorists targeted him during the COVID epidemic of 2020-2021, for instance. His association with disgraced financier Jeffrey Epstein apparently contributed to his divorce. Unlike Rockefeller, a committed Christian, Gates is agnostic.

Through it all, though, he has persisted. His foresight and business brilliance revolutionized the world. His philanthropic commitment to the poorest of the poor promises to continue remaking the world in generations to come.

Charles Schumer

Charles "Chuck" Schumer was born in Brooklyn, New York, in 1950, the son of Abraham and Selma Schumer. Abraham Schumer was an exterminator, and Selma was a homemaker. His family is Jewish, his ancestors immigrating to America from the city of Chortkiv in what is now western Ukraine. Chortkiv was an important center of Jewish life until the community was destroyed during the Holocaust.

Young Chuck was an outstanding student attending public schools in Brooklyn. As he neared high school graduation, he achieved a perfect score on the Scholastic Aptitude Test (SAT), a standardized exam given to American high school students preparatory to college admission. Schumer's fine grades and perfect SAT score opened the door for him to attend Harvard University in Cambridge, Massachusetts.

He was a chemistry major intent on a career in the sciences when he was swept up in the excitement of Senator Eugene McCarthy's insurgent campaign for president in 1968. The nation was convulsed at the time over the Vietnam War and civil rights. McCarthy challenged a sitting president from his own party, Lyndon B. Johnson.

McCarthy didn't win, but his abortive run set in motion a series of events that ended in Johnson dropping out of the race. After the murder of Senator Robert F. Kennedy, one of McCarthy's rivals for the nomination, the Democrats settled on Vice President Hubert Humphrey as their nominee during a tumultuous convention in Chicago. Humphrey lost the election in November to Richard Nixon.

Once bitten by the political bug, Schumer made it the center of his studies. After graduation, he attended Harvard Law School and passed the bar in New York State. He bypassed the practice of law, though, and went directly into politics. In his first campaign, he ran for and won a seat in the New York State Assembly in 1974, serving there until 1980.

In 1980, Schumer ran for the U. S. House of Representatives. He won that year the first of nine consecutive terms in the House, serving until 1998. At that point, he successfully challenged three-term Republican incumbent Alphonse D'Amato for the U. S. Senate, and holds the seat as of this writing.

Schumer's trademark has been his success in building consensus among his colleagues. He focuses particularly on the welfare of children and on health care reform. Part of his political practice is to visit each of New York's sixty-two counties each year, to better understand the needs of his constituents.

Schumer became Democratic Minority Leader in the Senate in 2021, the first Jewish person so chosen, and became Majority Leader when the Democrats won back the majority in 2023. He is pro-choice and, though he supports the American alliance with Israel, has been unafraid to criticize Israeli policies when he feels it is warranted.

His Senate colleagues tease him for being fond of publicity. Former Senator Bob Dole jokingly said, "The most dangerous place in Washington is between Charles Schumer and a television camera."

Schumer married in 1980 and is the father of two children. Teasing aside, he has been an effective advocate for his policies and party during his public life. Whether that is a good thing or not depends on one's political views.

Douglas Burgum

Douglas "Doug" Burgum entered life in Arthur, North Dakota, in 1956, one of three children born to Joseph and Katherine Burgum. His grandfather built a grain elevator in Arthur in 1906, going on to create a substantial agriculture business. Burgum's father died when Douglas was a freshman in high school.

After the trauma of his father's passing, Burgum completed high school and attended North Dakota State University, graduating in 1978. An outstanding student, he applied for and was accepted to study for a Master of Business Administration at Stanford University, finishing his degree in 1980.

After graduating, Burgum mortgaged farmland he owned to buy a stake in Great Plains Software in Fargo, North Dakota. He was highly successful, eventually buying the company outright. Under Burgum's leadership, the firm earned a place in the 1990s among the one hundred best places in the country to work, according to *Forbes* magazine.

Microsoft bought Burgum's company in 2001, and he became Senior Vice President of Microsoft Business Solutions. After stepping down from Microsoft in 2007, he ran an investment fund in his native North Dakota. In 2016, Burgum entered politics, running for and winning the governorship of his home State. Still in office at the time of this writing, he ranks among the wealthiest politicians in the United States.

Burgum, a noted conservative, is a staunch proponent of fossil fuels and an opponent of abortion rights. As governor, he signed one of the nation's most restrictive laws on abortion. After an abortive presidential run of his own, Burgum strongly supported Donald Trump's 2024 campaign for president, frequently being mentioned as Trump's potential running mate. In the end, Trump passed over him for vice president in favor of Ohio Senator J D Vance, instead appointing Burgum Secretary of the Interior.

By virtue of hard work and intelligence, Burgum turned a decent stake in an agricultural business into a vast personal fortune. He has invested part of that fortune in a political career, pursuing issues he believes are best for his State and nation.

Whether one approves of his positions or not, Burgum has proven unwilling to rest on his laurels. He has leveraged his success in pursuit of the greater good as he understands it, rather than solely for himself.

Eric Adams

Eric Leroy Adams came into this world in the Brownsville section of New York City in 1960. He is one of six children born to parents who migrated to New York from Alabama. His mother worked in housekeeping and his father was a butcher. The family's living circumstances were tenuous. They lived through eviction notices and the uncertainty that afflicts those near the bottom of the economic pile.

As a young teen, he joined a street gang and quickly ran afoul of the law. Taken into custody by the New York Police Department at 15, he alleges being beaten in the basement of a local precinct, an abuse that ended only when a Black cop intervened. He was then sent for a stint in a juvenile detention facility.

Whatever the details may have been, the incident focused young Eric's attention. With the help of a local Pentecostal pastor and encouragement from family, he took a different direction than the gang life that trapped so many around him. Adams graduated high school in the New York public schools and looked to a career in law enforcement. He hoped to improve outcomes for youngsters who, like himself, ran afoul of the law.

After graduating from the New York City Police Academy in 1984, he joined New York's transit police. When that unit merged with the New York City Police Department, Adams made the transition as well. His concern for effective policing across racial lines led him to work with the Nation of Islam, a controversial Black nationist group, because of the Nation's activity protecting New York housing projects. This and other controversial actions led to his retirement from the force after twenty-two years.

He then took his passion for racially-equitable policing and social justice into politics. After several unsuccessful campaigns, a party switch from Democrat to Republican and then back again, and more controversial comments, he was elected to the New York State Senate in 2007. He served until 2013, focusing his efforts on steering Black youth away from anti-social behavior and tempering law enforcement's actions toward them.

He won the Brooklyn Borough Presidency in a landslide in 2013, and was reelected by an even larger margin to it in 2017. While in office, he worked to improve educational opportunities in the community, all the while continuing his advocacy of effective, humane policing. During the COVID epidemic of 2020-2021, he often slept in his borough office to be available for the crisis situations that arose.

In 2021, Adams sought the Mayor's office in the city, running as a "new kind of Democrat": tough but fair on crime, proactive on education, and dedicated to economic development in blighted neighborhoods. He won, and took office as New York City's 110th Mayor in 2022.

Adams' tenure as Mayor has been filled with controversy, much like his working life before it. Accused of nepotism by his critics, his administration has suffered from a revolving-door turnover among its senior officials. Several of his deputies were ensnared in federal corruption investigations. In 2024, Adams himself faced a federal indictment on charges related to gifts and travel he had received from the Turkish government. The government alleged in his indictment that he had accepted bribes in exchange for easing Turkey's path to a new consulate in Manhattan. As of this writing, the case is unresolved.

Adams is in a domestic partnership, and has one child. For all the controversy, though, his life illustrates that in 21st Century America someone can still overcome hardship in young life, rise through intelligence and hard work, and make a significant difference in the world.

Juan Merchan

Juan Merchan came into the world in 1962 in Bogotá, the high mountain capital of Colombia, South America. The youngest of six children, he was six years old when his family moved to Queens, New York. Merchan became the first member of his family to attend college when he enrolled at Baruch College. After graduating there in 1990, he earned a law degree at Hofstra University in 1994.

Merchan cut his teeth as a prosecutor in the Manhattan District Attorney's office beginning in 1994, serving similar roles in other jurisdictions for twelve years. In 2006, New York City Mayor Michael Bloomberg appointed him as a judge in the New York City Family Court in the Bronx. Ann Pfau appointed him an acting judge in the city's criminal courts in 2009, where he remains as of this writing.

In that capacity, it fell to him to preside over the first criminal trial ever of a former US president when Donald Trump was indicted by the State of New York on 34 counts of falsifying business records. The jury found Trump guilty on all counts, but his reelection as president in 2024 put his sentencing on an indefinite hold.

Merchan remains the target of withering criticism from the former President and his supporters after the trial. It's worth pointing out that Merchan neither filed the charges against Trump, nor sought the case for his courtroom, nor deliberated with the jury on the verdict. He was, so it seems, just doing his job.

Sometimes, the exercise of Liberty is no fun at all.

Lawrence Watts

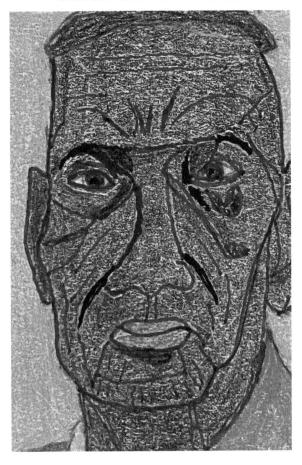

Lawrence Watts was born in 1924 to parents who left rural poverty in the American South and settled in Cleveland, Ohio. His family was part of a great migration of Blacks, weary of oppression and racism in the South, seeking better opportunities elsewhere in the United States. Watts's father found a job at Lincoln Electric, a major manufacturer of electronic components. His mother was a schoolteacher.

Watts attended Cleveland public schools, popular with his classmates and well-regarded by his teachers. He graduated high school in 1942, the first full year of America's involvement in World War II. Drafted into the U. S. Army, he trained as an aircraft mechanic and served three years with the mighty 8th Army Air Force in England.

After the war, he came home to Ohio, leveraging his air corps training and innate work ethic to a successful career. He settled near Cincinnati, Ohio, and spent his professional life at the General Electric aviation complex in Evendale, Ohio. Watts married in 1948. He and his wife settled down, bought a house, and raised three children in classic middle-America fashion. They and others anchored a thriving Black middle-class in staunchly egalitarian Ohio.

Though he had seen racism and discrimination elsewhere, the worst of those blights seemed to start across the Ohio River in Kentucky and get worse farther south. He knew at the time it was an enormous privilege to be watching the civil rights struggles on television, as if it were another country, instead of having to face it in person.

At age 100, still going strong, Watts is proud of the country he served and of the life he was able to build. He understands fully well that, but for an accident of birth, his struggle in his own country might have been significantly worse. He prays every single day for better outcomes in the generations to come.

Lidia Martinez

Lidia Martinez came into Liberty's dance in South Texas in 1938. Though her family had long resided there, the Texas political power structure had long disenfranchised them as a matter of policy. As a result, Lidia has spent the last thirty-five years working with the League of United Latin American Citizens (LULAC) to register legal residents to vote.

She answered a loud banging on her door at 6 AM on August 20, 2024. When she opened it, armed deputies stormed in, guns drawn and flashing warrants from the office of Texas Attorney General Ken Paxton. According to news reports, she spent several hours standing outside in her nightgown while officers searched her home and seized her computer, personal calendar, and certificate to conduct voter registration.

"They scared the hell out of me," she told reporters. "I feel that they're going to stop a lot of us from going out and doing our work, and that's what they want. I don't do anything illegal. I follow the rules of the elections office, and I have never done anything illegal."

State agents acted on a tip that Martinez and others had signed up persons illegally in the country as part of a vote-harvesting scheme. To date, the search has yielded no charges against her.

A San Antonio television outlet stated that, "To LULAC, these are intimidation tactics on the part of Attorney General Ken Paxton to suppress the Latino vote."

Paxton and others, of course, saw it as a necessary step to preserve election integrity. Ironically, Paxton's Republicans fared far better in the 2024 South Texas vote than expected. If LULAC engaged in vote-harvesting, it obviously did not work for Democrats.

"This is a free country," Ms. Martinez said. "This is not Russia."

Whether an indictment follows or not, the incident reminds us of the price many pay in the struggle for Liberty.

Rob Davis

Rob Davis, born in the Baby Boom in New York City, had a successful career in finance. Throughout his working life, he gave heavily of both his time and treasure to non-profits working with abused children. So consistent were his efforts for so long that he began to gain recognition for his ongoing support.

Davis didn't share his motivation until he was an old man in retirement. He revealed that he himself had been abused as a child. Though the perpetrator had long since died, the damage he felt inside could never be undone.

Furthermore, in the climate of his youth and young adulthood, children often weren't taken seriously when they claimed such things. They usually lacked the vocabulary to describe what was happening. If accusations were made, the cultural mores of the time generally swept them under the rug, as the saying goes, to hide them from others. As the heartbreaking stories which emerged later about clergy sexual abuse illustrate, the problem was real, as was the tendency to cover it up.

Davis knew he could do nothing to rectify what had happened to him. What he could do was to invest his money and effort into helping children going through the same things in the present. This is exactly what he dedicated his lifelong labor to do.

Rob Davis couldn't help all the children in need, he knew. But he refused to let that be an excuse for helping none at all.

Sometimes, the only thing we are at Liberty to do is help others.

Julio Morales

Julio Morales's family arrived in what is now New Mexico in 1694, a few years after Spanish authorities suppressed the Pueblo Revolt.

Julio, following his family's long tradition of public service, earned a Civil Engineering degree from the University of New Mexico in Albuquerque, the State's largest city.

He spent his working life as an engineer for the New Mexico Department of Transportation, building and repairing highways.

Every now and then, someone passing him in construction zones will honk, flip him off, and curse him for being an illegal alien.

Doris Little

Doris Little, "Sister Doris" to those she loves, has spent much of the last fifty years loving her church and its children in the Smithfield neighborhood of Birmingham, Alabama. Rain or shine, summer or winter, she's always there.

Any children who walk through the door become her children while they are there. She loves them, teaches them, feeds them, prays with them, and keeps up with them.

Their troubles become her troubles.

She doesn't do it because she has to. She does it because she loves the Lord and finds her joy in children.

Sometimes, cynical people don't understand that, and they question her motives.

She does it anyway.

The best vote of confidence in what she does comes from the children themselves. They vote with their feet and keep coming to church.

Liberty, it seems, is perfected in love.

Sean Penn

Sean Penn, an American actor and activist, was born in Santa Monica, California, in 1960, to Leo Penn and Eileen Ryan, both actors. He made his first uncredited TV appearance in 1974 in an episode of *Little House on the Prairie*, his first credited part coming in 1979.

Penn's talent came to the fore early on. He rose to movie stardom in *Taps* in 1981, becoming a Hollywood heartthrob in the 1980s. Penn's passion was not limited to acting. He has spent his life and career in the presence of physically beautiful people, marrying three times. His marriages to Madonna, Robin Wright, and Leila George all ended in divorce.

As his fame grew in Hollywood, Penn became an activist. He vocally criticized the administration of President George W. Bush, and built relationships with American adversaries Fidel Castro of Cuba and Hugo Chavez of Venezuela. Penn worked intensely on relief projects following Hurricane Katrina in 2005 and the catastrophic Haitian earthquake of 2011. In 2015, he arranged a surreptitious interview with notorious Mexican drug lord Joaquin Guzmán, known as "El Chapo." Since 2022, he has supported Ukrainian President Volodymyr Zelenskyy as Ukraine resists a Russian invasion.

Through it all, his acting burned bright. Penn has won two Oscars, a Golden Globe, and two Critics' Choice Awards for his acting to date, as well as many other honors. He seems to have successfully transitioned from "young and hunky" to "old and rugged" with his star power intact. Despite his evident talent, many criticize him harshly for what they consider his ill-advised activism and abuse of his celebrity platform.

Penn has had anger-management issues over the years. He was arrested multiple times in the 1980s for assaulting journalists, paparazzi, and romantic rivals. He served two jail stints in the early 1990s, one for assaulting a worker on a movie set, and the other for reckless driving. As recently as 2010, Penn pleaded no contest to another assault charge. He was sentenced to anger management classes and community service.

However, Penn has never been arrested for domestic violence. When a Hollywood director in 2015 insinuated he had, lumping him together with other known abusers in a public statement, Penn sued for defamation. The director apologized and withdrew the statement, and Penn dropped the lawsuit.

Through it all, he remains Sean Penn, unmistakably himself: a talented, passionate man, committed to making a difference in the world in more than just acting. Love him or hate him, he refuses to take justice for granted, and he manifestly does not fear standing up to the powerful for what he considers right.

Jack Teich

Jack Teich was 34-year-old, married father of two when he was kidnapped at gunpoint from his Long Island, New York, driveway in 1974. He had just arrived home from work at an architectural supply company owned by his family, but was taken before he could enter the house.

Teich's family reported him missing later that evening, but didn't suspect kidnapping until his captors began calling with ransom demands. The Teiches worked closely with the FBI and the New York police, negotiating a ransom of $750,000. Hoping against hope, they placed the ransom according to the kidnappers' instruction in a locker at Penn Station. The captors then released Teich, but law enforcement lost track of the man who retrieved the money from the locker in the crowd at the station.

After a year of investigation, the FBI arrested Richard Williams, a Black radical, after tracing money used for the ransom. With a search warrant, they found $38,000 more hidden in the wall of Williams' mobile home in California. Not long after, they arrested Charles Berkley, a former employee of Teich's company who had provided Williams with inside information.

Williams was convicted and served twenty years in prison before his conviction was overturned on a technicality. Berkley, though arrested, was never charged. Fifty years after the fact, the bulk of the ransom money has not been recovered.

It remains one of the few such cases in which the victim lived to tell his story. Teich remains obsessive fifty years later about locking doors and securing spaces. The trauma of the Liberty taken violently from him as a young man has cast its shadow over the rest of his life.

Swami Sarvapriyananda

Swami Sarvapriyananda was born Biswarup Palit to a religious Hindu family in Kolkata, India, in 1971. As a young man, he completed a degree at the Xavier Institute of Management in India, before committing fully to the religious life.

Two of his childhood religious heroes were Sri Ramakrishna and Swami Vivekananda. Ramakrishna was a 19th Century Hindu mystic and holy man, and Vivekananda was his principal disciple. Vivekananda traveled in 1893 from British India to the United States to address the World Parliament of Religions in Chicago, the first interfaith gathering of its kind.

He established the Vedanta Society of New York in 1894 and the Vedanta Society of San Francisco in 1900.

Biswarup Palit joined the Ramakrishna Order in 1994 and took monastic vows as a *sannyasa* ten years later. Following the local custom, he received the title "Swami" and took the name "Sarvapriyananda" at his ordination. A *sannyasa* renounces material possessions and pleasures, cultivates detachment from worldly affairs, and pursues a peaceful life. "Swami" is a rough equivalent of "Reverend" in the West, indicative of one set apart for a religious vocation. Roughly translated, "Sarvapriyananda" means "All beloved bliss."

Following his monastic vows, Swami Sarvapriyananda served in a variety of roles within the Ramakrishna Order in India, teaching inquirers and taking part in educational life. He immigrated to the United States in 2015 to serve as an Assistant Minister at the Vedanta Society of Southern California. In 2017, he moved to the East Coast to serve as the Resident Minister and director of the Vedanta Society of New York.

Since his move to New York, Swami Sarvapriyananda has gained a substantial following through skillful use of various online video platforms. He is, in his own way, one fruit of religious Liberty in the United States.

Kenneth Boozer

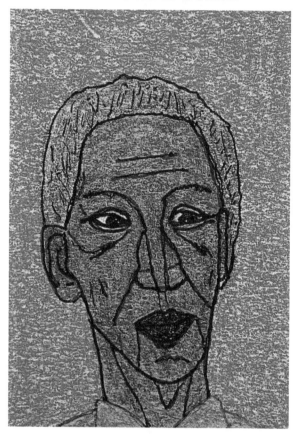

Kenneth Boozer's family became some of the first Black residents of the Sunnyside neighborhood of Houston in the late 1930s. They came from Waller County, Texas, northwest of Houston, drawn by the industrial jobs springing up on the east side of the city.

Kenneth is the youngest of five brothers and the only one born in Houston. His mother, Joseelee, gave birth to him at home, in the house where he lived most of his life. He does not know his father's name. As the youngest child, he took care of his mother until her passing.

During his teenage years, the crack epidemic raged in the rugged southeastern neighborhoods of Houston. He was by no means immune from it, though he avoided the worst ravages it inflicted on others. He recalled many years later that of all the peer group he grew up with in Sunnyside, only two were not either in prison or dead.

Kenneth escaped that fate in a grueling manner. As a teenage hellraiser, he was in a car full of other teens up to no good when they were in a serious wreck. His neck was broken. Though he was not paralyzed, he had to spend a year in recovery, his neck brace held in place by screws drilled in his skull.

When he recovered sufficiently, he made a point to stay out of cars driven by drugged-out youths, and found a job at a church. In his late twenties, disgust over what was happening in his neighborhood and his own role in it led to a profound repentance. Kenneth came to Christian faith in the depths of his despair, was baptized, and made a new start in life.

Now in his sixties, he continues working at the church where he first found a job. His kindness and love for others, and their love for him in turn, continue. Sometimes, in Liberty's dance, what seems like terrible luck can turn out for the good when conscience, faith, and second chances are possible.

Maurie McInnis, Ph. D.

Maurie McInnis was born in Florida in the mid-1960s to academically gifted parents. The family moved to Knoxville, Tennessee, where both parents taught at the flagship University of Tennessee. She attended the elite Webb School there, graduating in 1984.

McInnis finished an undergraduate degree in 1990 in Art History at the University of Virginia in Charlottesville. She continued her studies at Yale University, earning her Ph.D. in 1996.

After distinguishing herself academically studying "the politics of art and slavery in the American South," according to her biography at Yale, she moved into academic administration. She served at James Madison University, the University of Virginia, the University of Texas, and Stony Brook University. In 2024, she became Yale's first non-interim female president, and the 24th president overall in the illustrious history of the institution.

McInnis is a fourth-generation educator, having risen in her career through leading institutions to the top of ultra-elite Yale. Her first year on campus coincided with sharp protests against Israel's war against Gaza and outbreaks of anti-semitism on campus.

Kaylee Frederick

Kaylee Frederick, who came into this world in the mid-1960s, became vaguely aware around the 4th grade that her long blonde hair, deep blue eyes, and thin figure drew attention from the boys. She felt strangely indifferent to it, though her female friends, even at that age, were envious.

She lived in Baytown, Texas, an eastern suburb of Houston built around an enormous Exxon refinery. Kaylee's father was plant operator until his mid-50s, when the company pensioned him off for a younger, less expensive replacement. It was their standard practice. When Kaylee started Middle School, her mother went back to work part-time at a store in San Jacinto Mall.

An only child, Kaylee's life outside of school revolved around the massive

First Baptist Church on the north side of town, where her parents were members. The church emphasized purity to its youth and children, and conservative politics to its adults. Kaylee put on a "purity ring" as a thirteen-year-old, part of a program encouraging teens to remain virgins until marriage.

She sensed that many of her friends took the whole purity issue as a joke. For her, it was an excuse to keep the boys who circled around her with hungry eyes at arm's length. At slumber parties with other girls in the youth group, when they shared giggling stories of crushes and boys, Kaylee laughed along with them. She wondered to herself, though, why she never felt such things.

At sixteen, she met Cindi, a new girl at school, at a church-sponsored prayer event around the school flag pole. She was smitten, but didn't realize it. In her world of purity, having feelings for another girl didn't enter her awareness.

The girls became fast friends, however. Whenever Cindi agreed to a sleepover, Kaylee noticed her own pulse racing, her hands sweating, and her face becoming flushed. Of course, nothing sexual ever happened or was even contemplated in their time alone.

Two years later, Cindi left for Texas Tech in Lubbock, and Kaylee remained in town, living in the dorm at Lee College. Feeling restless without knowing why one day, she flipped on the TV absently. A black-clad Joan Jett was singing *I Love Rock'n'Roll* on MTV.

Transfixed, she stared at the woman on screen. Her heart raced, her palms sweat, and her face grew flushed. She began to tremble, and then it hit her like a bolt from heaven. She liked girls! Despite all the warnings, all the purity rings, all the preemptive denunciations, she liked girls! No, she LOVED girls! She realized that moment that she felt for girls what she had never remotely felt for any boy ever.

She longed, burned, and lusted in that moment for Joan Jett, but more than that, for Cindi. She brushed away in her mind with heated disdain what she knew her church and parents would say. Life started anew for Kaylee in that moment. She felt Liberty in a way she never had before, even though she admitted to herself she had no idea what she'd do with it.

Andrew Mickton

Andrew Mickton, born in a northeastern suburb of Fort Worth, Texas, in the mid-1960s, knew from early childhood he wasn't like the other boys around him. He was the only child of older parents. He was not fond of the sports that fascinated boys of his age, was always the last person picked during gym class, and suffered frequently from bullies.

Andrew was gifted in math. His parents both worked in highly technical fields, and their son became an early adopter of the personal computer as that technology began revolutionizing the American economy in the late

1970s. He brought his formidable skill set into that field both during and after his college days.

Andrew was precocious in other ways as well. His unease with typical male pursuits during childhood coupled with the growing community he found through his interests in computing. He realized he was gay while still a teen. This realization, coming as it did in the aftermath of the Stonewall riots in New York and the increasing visibility of queer culture in American life, led him into the heart of the Montrose neighborhood in Houston.

The flourishing lifestyle of those early years soon led to backlashes, of course. Homosexuality became a lightning rod in the nation's politics at the time. Even deadlier, the AIDS epidemic soon exploded, driven particularly among young gay men by unsafe sexual practices. Before AIDS, gay men laughed at the notion of having to use a condom.

After several years in Houston and dozens of deaths among his friends, he relocated to the Bay Area of California. His body held out long enough for him to see the advent of anti-retroviral medications, which ultimately kept his HIV infection at bay. At the same time, his intellectual gifts and mathematical skills proved enormously lucrative. He then began to push the boundaries of tattooing and body modification.

Mickton remains in California, in a world far removed from the redneck Texas suburb on his childhood. He found early on Liberty to be who he was, despite cultural disdain. Through a combination of medical breakthroughs and his own place at the forefront of the computer revolution, he's been able to live a life few could conceive of in his native culture.

He acknowledges that, though he has enjoyed Liberty, his pursuit of happiness, of intimate love, has not been as successful.

Patricia Fowler

Patricia Fowler, born in Warren, Pennsylvania, in the 1970s, never expected to be part of a controversy. She grew up during the deindustrialization of the area, as one-time manufacturers closed their factories and the local economy declined.

Patricia's parents were public employees, though, and managed to survive the economic decline around them. Patricia's decision to apply for a government job after junior college was not controversial.

She spent twenty years in the office of the Election Clerk, learning the intricacies of the system that existed in Warren County. When the elected clerk decided to retire, it made sense that Patricia, the most experienced employee in the office, should run to succeed him.

She did, winning office in 2018 and anticipating a peaceful retirement in a few years. It didn't work out that way. Pennsylvania had become a swing State with Donald Trump's victory in the 2016 presidential election. It swung back in 2020 when Trump lost to Joe Biden.

Trump refused to acknowledge his defeat in 2020, either in Pennsylvania or nationwide, alleging massive fraud. Though the election in Warren County had gone smoothly, Fowler found herself the target of hostile allegations by Trump's furious supporters. To her astonishment, a handful even of long-time acquaintances in the county lobbed such accusations at her. The same pattern repeated itself in many American swing States.

As the 2024 election season heated up, accusations, verbal attacks, and threats of actual violence piled up in heated Pennsylvania, one of the most important of the swing States. The local sheriff detailed deputies to extra security at the elections office and ballot boxes.

Patricia Fowler, who never wanted to do anything other than finish her career doing a job she had done well for decades, never imagined becoming an object of hate for doing it. She gives serious thought to resigning the office and getting out of the spotlight, despite the mess doing so would make of her retirement.

In the event, though, the 2024 election ended without major controversy.

Linda Sun

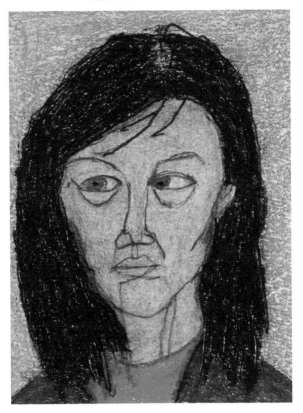

Linda Sun, born in Nanjing, China, in 1983, immigrated with her parents to the United States when she was five. She became a naturalized U. S. citizen after completing the legal requirements.

Sun earned an undergraduate degree at Barnard College and a masters degree at Columbia University in New York, then entered political life advocating diversity, equity, and inclusion for the Chinese minority. She served the administration of New York Governor Andrew Cuomo as a deputy diversity officer, then served his successor, Kathy Hochul, as a deputy chief of staff.

In 2024, she was charged along with her husband, Chris Hu, as being an unregistered agent of the Chinese government, following an FBI investigation. Among the alleged crimes in the indictment were censoring criticism of China's actions against its Uighur minority, preventing meetings with Taiwanese officials, and abusing her position to invite Chinese officials to important New York business conferences.

According to United States Attorney Breon Peace, who brought the charges, "As alleged, while appearing to serve the people of New York as Deputy Chief of Staff within the New York State Executive Chamber, the defendant and her husband actually worked to further the interests of the Chinese government and the CCP." ("CCP" is the Chinese Communist Party.) Attorney Peace went on to say, "The illicit scheme enriched the defendant's family to the tune of millions of dollars."

In the United States, persons are considered innocent until proven guilty in a court of law. As of this writing, that has still not happened. Nevertheless, the case raises issues about misusing Liberty to advance the interests of hostile powers.

Maria Jose Sandoval

Born in Mexico, Maria Jose Sandoval Torrijo crossed the U. S. border illegally as a teenager in 1998 seeking higher-paying work than was available at home. She purchased a fraudulent Social Security number through a black market broker, and secured a job. She works diligently and pays into the Social Security system, though she will never receive payments from it. After all, the Social Security number she uses is not hers.

Her children were born in Dallas, Texas, and are American citizens by birth, as guaranteed by the Fourteenth Amendment to the U. S. Constitution. That amendment, passed in 1868, makes almost all those born on U. S. soil citizens automatically. It was crafted during post-Civil War Reconstruction to secure citizenship rights for persons freed from slavery, who were often denied civil rights on the allegation that they had not been U. S. citizens.

Many U. S. residents today find themselves in a similar bind to Sandoval. Though they work and contribute to the economy and their U. S.-born children are citizens, they are nevertheless here illegally and subject to arrest and deportation at any time.

Maria Jose lives in the shadows, so to speak. Her presence and that of many like her is actually a crucial cog in the health of the economic machine. It keeps labor costs low and subsidizes federal benefits, and cynical businesses often enable the undocumented flow. Keeping the supply of labor high drives down their production costs, depressing wages of others working in similar jobs.

Despite being the proverbial "nation of immigrants," the United States has long struggled to deal coherently with the issue. Should Maria Jose be deported? If so, what will happen to her children who are citizens by birth? How will the economy cope if substantial numbers of lower-wage workers are expelled from the country in a short period of time? This concern presses particularly, since undocumented workers perform most agricultural and food processing labor.

Those questions, though, seem to be for more affluent people to dispute. For her part, Maria Jose continues bussing tables, washing dishes, and cleaning floors, providing for loved ones here and in Mexico as she does so.

Elisa Moreno Goya

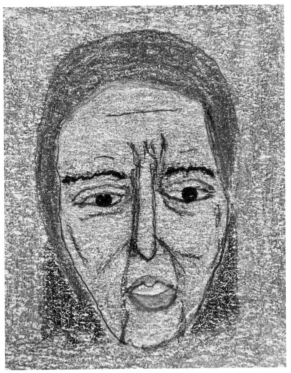

Elisa Moreno Goya was 18 and pregnant in crime-ridden Medellín, Colombia, when her child's father was gunned down in cartel-related violence there. She gave birth to a girl a few months later, living on her own in poverty in the city. Though family lived nearby, they were not in a position to help.

Elisa, a bright, attractive young woman, set her sights on getting out of Colombia and into the United States. The overland trek to the U. S. border through the Darién Gap, Central America, and Mexico rightly scared even a woman of her own fortitude. She researched other possibilities and found marital agencies specializing in matching Colombian women with American men.

The risks were obvious. Some of the women were trafficked when they reached the U. S. Some of the men were complete losers who, unable to find or keep American wives, preferred to purchase Colombian ones on the black market. Elisa was enough of a realist to understand the situation. She was hard-headed enough to believe she could make it work for herself and her daughter.

She signed up with an agency and began enduring what the other women referred to as "cattle calls" when Americans came to visit. Stephen, a forty-something bachelor from northern Alabama, made a passable impression a few months later. She latched ahold and convinced him in short order to get married. It was the reason he'd come there, he reasoned. Why not?

Elisa's family expressed extreme skepticism, naturally enough, but the young woman insisted she knew what she was doing. Stephen applied on her behalf for a fiancée visa, which allowed her to skip to the head of the line of other Colombians hoping come to the U. S.. Her daughter would be allowed to accompany her as well.

To her quiet amazement and satisfaction, things actually worked out the way she planned. The man paid for her travel and brought her to Alabama, where the two married. She and her daughter stayed with him for two years, long enough for her to feel she had satisfied some sort of moral debt to him. It was also long enough to convince the immigration authorities she had married in good faith.

She passed the time working at a local restaurant, setting her money aside and taking care of her daughter. She took great care during the period not to get pregnant.

After two years, she took her child and the money she'd saved and, while Stephen was at work, got on the bus to Atlanta. Mother and daughter arrived in the city and settled into a small apartment she had prearranged with a friend. Elisa then informed Stephen of their whereabouts and well-being. Heartbroken, he pleaded for her to return. She didn't.

A Spanish-speaking lawyer in Atlanta helped her get a divorce and protect her immigration status. Three years later, having fulfilled the residency requirement, Elisa Moreno Goya applied for citizenship. She passed the test, took the oath, and left the building, tiny flag in hand, as a newly minted American.

Walking out into the Atlanta sunshine that day, she felt for the first time in many years a giddy, almost childlike excitement about the future.

Sydney Lemmon

Sydney Lemmon, born in 1990 in Los Angeles, is an American actor. She grew up in Connecticut, studied acting at Boston University, and earned a Master of Fine Arts (MFA) degree from Yale University in 2017. Her parents are Chris Lemmon and Gina Raymond, both actors, and her grandfather was famed American actor Jack Lemmon. She comes by her passion for dramatic arts naturally.

Lemmon's first credited role, according to the Internet Movie Database (IMDb), was a highly regarded comedy called *Badpuss: A Popumentary*, in 2014. Publicists described it as, "An honest and hilarious look at the music industry through the eyes of an all-girl rock band."

Several smaller roles followed, among them a guest appearance on *Fear the*

Walking Dead in 2019, for which she earned a Saturn Award nomination as "Best Guest Performance in a Television Series." She was cast as the lead in *Helstrom* in 2020, and guest-starred to rave reviews in *Succession*.

In 2024, Lemmon enjoyed what the New York Times called a "breakout role" on Broadway in *Job*, a play about "a content moderator having a mental breakdown."

Sydney Lemmon, latest iteration of a famous show business family, is a leading voice in Liberty's next phase on stage and on screen.

Ian Stein

Ian Stein's great-grandparents escaped a pogrom in 1905 in what was then still the Russian Empire. They made their way with other Jewish refugees to New York City. The Steins were hard-working people and, despite their immigrant status and lack of English, soon carved out a decent living in the Crown Heights neighborhood of Brooklyn.

Ian's grandfather, Sherman Stein, was born in 1915, the last of six children. Like his parents, he was diligent in his work, which led him in turn to success in school and college. He finished in the late 1930s, at a time when the entire family often gathered around the radio, listening to terrifying developments in Europe.

Sherman became an officer in the U. S. Army after Pearl Harbor. He served in George Patton's U. S. Third Army, in its smashing offensives, fighting his way across France and into southern Germany by the end of the war. He was nearby in April 1945, when American units overran the concentration camp at Buchenwald.

This season of horror, the realization of what supposedly civilized Germans had done to his own Jewish people, shook Sherman to the core. He survived the war and returned to America to the sickening confirmation that none of his family members in Eastern Europe had survived the Holocaust. Sherman's trauma led him to a highly ethical atheism for the rest of his life. "How could there be a God," he would say in genuine anguish, "if things like that happen?"

Yet America was different. Sherman relocated to Houston after the war, where he raised his family When he held his sixth grandson, Ian, in his arms in the early 1990s, he tried hard to believe that being a Jew in Houston was no more controversial than being a Presbyterian or a Methodist.

Ian, raised in confident assimilation in cosmopolitan Houston, rarely gave his Jewishness a second thought. Anti-semitism was yesterday's problem. Yet there were disturbing upticks of anti-Jewish violence in his twenties.

It hit home for him in 2018. He was dating a Jewish woman whose family was still religious. His girlfriend's grandmother, attending Shabbat services as always in a synagogue in Pittsburgh, was seriously wounded in a mass shooting carried out by a violent anti-semite. "Why would someone shoot a harmless old lady?" Ian agonized to himself afterward.

More violence and shootings followed, along with warnings from authorities to Jewish communities. Ian, now married, woke up on October 7, 2023, to news of Hamas's murderous rampage in Israel. 1,200 were murdered and 250 were kidnapped, the most gruesome violence against Jews since the Holocaust. Israel's counterattack against Hamas and

Hezbollah followed.

As the war dragged on, Ian found himself in anti-semitic crosshairs in his job at a local university. Anti-Zionist protesters screamed obscenities at him repeatedly when they saw the Star of David pendant he had worn on a chain around his neck since childhood. An ancient dread he'd sensed in his grandparents and dismissed as obsolete reared its ugly head in his life.

This man, the fourth generation in the land of Liberty, suddenly felt his assumptions of acceptance and safety crumbling. Jews, even non-practicing ones, were once again far more controversial than Presbyterians and Methodists, through no choice of their own.

Where is Liberty in a climate of fear?

Daisy Alioto

Born in Massachusetts in the early 1990s, Daisy Alioto possessed a precocious brilliance that set her apart from many of her peers. She finished an award-winning undergraduate degree at Bowdoin College and followed it up with internships and writing jobs at several of the luminous names in contemporary American media.

She took stock of the way that streaming services and so-called new media were rapidly pushing aside legacy media and traditional forms of publishing. This led her to a full embrace of the new forms. She publishes an online newsletter and runs a publishing company while continuing to write for older outlets.

Alioto is one of the leading faces of Liberty's self-expression in the 21st Century.

Guillermo Salinas

Guillermo Salinas is the seven-year-old grandson of a woman who fraudulently used a fiancée visa to enter the United States. His mother, too, was born outside of the country, and piggybacked on her mother's "green card," legal residence, to secure her own status. She gave birth to Guillermo at 16.

Guillermo is a birthright citizen of the United States, having been born on U. S. soil. A first grader, his teachers describe him as a happy boy and a middling student. He loves video games, dinosaurs, and playing soccer.

He has no inkling that his home and family are anything less than secure, or that it could all change in an instant.

Peace Out!

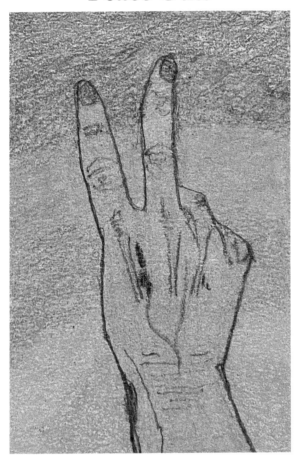

Take a deep breath!
Peace out!
Find little compassion!
Give the momentary benefit of a doubt!
What's it gonna hurt?

The Liberty Tree Reconsidered

Liberty means the ability to make our own life decisions according to our own sense of what is best.

Of course, we face pre-existing limits on that Liberty. None of us chooses to be born, after all. Though we may hasten it or, perhaps, postpone it by choices we make, none of us escapes death either. Our Liberty, under the best circumstances, is partial, dependent on much that is beyond our control. But within those limits, Liberty abides.

We recognize it most clearly when it is denied. Many of those in this book were denied Liberty, often brutally. Though we cannot go back and change their experiences, we can more fully appreciate our right to choose in light of their lack of the same.

As we've also seen in the book, Liberty does not guarantee us an easy path. Some of those whose stories we've told spent their Liberty doing difficult service for others. Some, having received it, longed quietly for those days when others made decisions for them. We are at Liberty to fail as well as to succeed. Most times, we fall somewhere in between.

But Liberty has been a driving force in America throughout our history. We can trace its progress in these pages, as well as its setbacks. We have historically built toward a society that allows individuals to make their own choices, within the boundaries of law, common sense, and decency. The best test of our progress is the extent we provide the greatest Liberty to the widest range of persons among us. Race, gender, class, and inclinations are secondary to that.

The Liberty Tree near the Boston Common is long since gone, but the Liberty Tree as an ideal lives on among us. It too goes through its seasons: green shoots in spring, growth in summer, leaves falling in autumn, life drawn within itself in winter.

As long as we safeguard it, it will abide. It has deep, deep roots in its native soil. To keep our Liberty, we have to help others keep theirs too. Sometimes, others exercise Liberty in ways we like, and that makes it easy. Sometimes, they don't, though, and that's when the project becomes demanding.

If someone exercises their Liberty in a way that doesn't harm me in mine or impose a non-consensual harm on others, I believe we must respect it. People at Liberty disagree on many things. Yet free societies impose themselves only where life and well-being are at stake.

This is a hard road sometimes, yet living in a place without such Liberty is much worse. Ask Simon Dansk, Samuel Sharpe, or Jack Teich, whose stories appear in this book.

We can't keep Liberty from being a double-edged sword sometimes, either.

It is Liberty both to thrive and to fail. If we move too far to ensure against failure, Liberty disappears. If we don't move at all to cushion the worst of failure, society becomes brutal and uncaring.

As with so many things, how well Liberty works comes down to us. What will we do with the ability to make our own life decisions according to our own sense of what is best?

Will we maintain a positive attitude toward it? Will we persist in it, even when it doesn't go our way? Will we take risks for it, as so many have before us?

More than anything else, these things will determine whether Liberty is a blessing in our own lives or not. In honor of all those in this book, I hope it will be.

Places Mentioned In Order
of Appearance

Kitty Unami
Boston
Massachusetts Bay Colony
England
The Atlantic Ocean
Oklahoma
Conrad Heyer
Germany
London
Massachusetts
Dorchester Heights, Massachusetts
The Mason-Dixon Line
Delaware
The Delaware River
New York
Pennsylvania
New Jersey
Trenton, New Jersey
Simon Dansk
St. Jan Island,
The Danish West Indies
Africa
Europe
The Caribbean Sea
Denmark
The United States
Nancy Daniels
Barbados Island
The West Indies
The British Empire
Shapley Ross
Texas
Kentucky
Missouri

Milam County, Texas
Austin, Texas
Waco, Texas
Jack Merrifield
The Trinity River
Oak Cliff, Texas
Dallas, Texas
Samuel Sharpe
Jamaica
Will Turner
North Carolina
New Hampshire
John Watson
Tennessee
The Tennessee River
Arkansas
Pine Bluff, Arkansas
Rusk County, Texas
Mary Thompson
Alabama
Sojourner Truth
Ulster County, New York
New York City
Akron, Ohio
Michigan
Battle Creek, Michigan
Abraham Lincoln
Indiana
Illinois
Springfield, Illinois
South Carolina
Fort Sumter, South Carolina
Maryland
Antietam, Maryland

Marcel Fauvrot
Louisiana
New Orleans
Chalmette, Louisiana
John Bell Hood
Owingsville, Kentucky
West Point, New York
California
Virginia
Gettysburg, Pennsylvania
Chickamauga, Tennessee
Georgia
Atlanta, Georgia
Franklin, Tennessee
Mississippi
Tom Southwell
The Oregon Trail
The Mississippi River
Oregon
The West Coast
Nebraska
Colorado
Jim Watson
Pea Ridge, Arkansas
Nathan Bedford Forrest
Fort Pillow, Tennessee
Selma, Alabama
Nashville, Tennessee
Memphis, Tennessee
Elijah Adams
Georgia
Bejamin "Pap" Singleton
Davidson County, Tennessee
Canada
Ontario, Canada
Michigan
Detroit, Michigan
Kansas City, Missouri
Al Smith
The Rio Grande River

John Henry Smith
Pike County, Alabama
Troy, Alabama
Montgomery, Alabama
Shiloh, Tennessee
Vicksburg, Mississippi
Alton Beard
Saint Louis, Missouri
Bethany, Missouri
James Beckwourth
The Rocky Mountains
The Sierra Nevada Mountains
Nevada
Reno, Nevada
Montana
Fort Smith, Montana
Ginny Scott
Cincinnati, Ohio
Bridget "Biddy" Mason
Utah
Los Angeles, California
George Washington Carver
Diamond, Missouri
Neosho, Missouri
Tuskegee, Alabama
Sweden
John D. Rockefeller
Richford, New York
Kykuit, Westchester County,
New York
The Philippines
Claude McKay
Charleston, South Carolina
The Soviet Union
Paris, France
Harlem, New York
Chicago, Illinois
"Blind Tom" Wiggins
The White House

William Casby
Danville, Virginia
Algiers, Louisiana
Lila Johnson
Shreveport, Louisiana
Clara Brim
Plaquemine Bouley, Acadia,
Beaumont, Texas
Mary Estelle
Natchez, Mississippi
"Old Man" Elkins
The Texas Panhandle
Fanny Moore
Shenandoah Valley, Virginia
Presley Campbell
Malakoff, Texas
Hawkins, Texas
Samuel Langhorne Clemens
Florida, Missouri
Spain
Connecticut
Paul Laurence Dunbar
Dayton, Ohio
Washington, D.C.
Wanada Parker Page
Indian Territory
Fort Parker, Texas
Fort Sill, Oklahoma
Lawton, Oklahoma
George Washington Cavin
Springfield, Missouri
Nacogdoches, Texas
Nivac, Texas
Jasper, Texas
The Gulf of Mexico
Louis Armstrong
Lithuania
Ernie Dawkins
Baltimore, Maryland

Zora Neale Hurston
Notalsuga, Alabama
Florida
Eatonville, Florida
Gwendolyn Elizabeth Brooks
Topeka, Kansas
Ralph Ellison
Oklahoma City, Oklahoma
Cab Calloway
Rochester, New York
The Cotton Club,
Harlem, New York
Hollywood, California
Iosefa Fa'atiu
Tutuila Island
Samoa
The Pacific Ocean
New England
Pago Pago, Samoa
New Zealand
Pearl Harbor, Hawaii
Ralph Mulally
West Virginia
Melvin Reese
Polk County, Florida
The Seminole Reservation, Florida
Bartow, Florida
River Rouge, Michigan
Joseph Bonnano
Italy
Sicity, Italy
Cuba
Arizona
Luis Tiant, Sr.
Havana, Cuba
Veracruz, Mexico
Francis Albert Sinatra
Hoboken, New Jersey
Las Vegas, Nevada

Judy Tyler
Wyoming
George Cunyus
Korea
Ben Kelley
San Angelo, Texas
Mary Ellen Faust
Decatur, Illinois
Waldron, Arkansas
Tyler, Texas
Joe Cornelius
Minden, Louisiana
Bob Newhart
Oak Park, Illinois
Houston, Texas
The Tidelands Motel,
Houston, Texas
Shelley Duvall
Fort Worth, Texas
Tsung-Dao Lee
Shanghai, China
The Yellow Sea
Guizhou, China
Luis Tiant, Jr.
Mexico
George H. W. Bush
Chichijima, Pacific Theater
Midland, Texas
Iraq
Kuwait
Nancy Pelosi
The Bay Area, California
Ukraine
San Francisco, California
Rupert Murdoch
Australia
Melbourne, Australia
Rudolph Giuliani
Brooklyn, New York

Joe Biden
Scranton, Pennsylvania
Newcastle County, Delaware
Donald Trump
Queens, New York
Bill Gates
Seattle, Washington
Washington (State)
Charles Schumer
Chorkiv, Ukraine
Israel
Douglas Burgum
North Dakota
Arthur, North Dakota
Fargo, North Dakota
Eric Adams
Brownsville Neighborhood,
New York City
Turkey
Juan Merchan
Colombia, South America
Bogotá, Colombia
The Bronx, New York
Lawrence Watts
Cleveland, Ohio
Evendale, Ohio
The Ohio River
Lidia Martinez
South Texas
San Antonio, Texas
Russia
Julio Morales
New Mexico
Albuquerque, New Mexico
Doris Little
Birmingham, Alabama
Sean Penn
Santa Monica, California
Venezuela
Haiti

Jack Teich
Long Island, New York
Penn Station, New York City
Swami Sarvapriyananda
Kolkata, India
Southern California
Kenneth Boozer
Sunnyside Neighborhood,
Houston, Texas
Waller County, Texas
Maurie McInnis
Knoxville, Tennessee
Gaza
Kaylee Frederick
Baytown, Texas
Andrew Mickton
Montrose Neighborhood,
Houston, Texas

Patricia Fowler
Warren, Pennsylvania
Linda Sun
Nanjing, China
Xinjiang, China
Taiwan
Elisa Moreno Goya
Medellín, Colombia
Ian Stein
Crown Heights Neighborhood,
Brooklyn, New York
Buchenwald, Germany
Pittsburgh, Pennsylvania

Religious Institutions Mentioned

Educational Institutions Mentioned

Baylor University
Waco, Texas
**The Agricultural and Mechanical
College of Texas**
(later Texas A&M University)
College Station, Texas
U. S. Military Academy
West Point, New York
Wilberforce College
(later Wilberforce University)
Wilberforce, Ohio
Iowa State College
(later Iowa State University)
Ames, Iowa
Tuskegee Institute
(later Tuskegee University),
Tuskegee, Alabama
The University of Chicago
Chicago, Illinois
Kansas State College (later
Kansas State University)
Manhattan, Kansas
Boston College
Boston, Massachusetts
Jarvis Christian College
(later Jarvis Christian University)
Hawkins, Texas
Dayton High School
Dayton, Ohio
Howard University
Washington, D.C.
Chiloco Indian School
Newkirk, Oklahoma
Carlisle Indian School
Carlisle, Pennsylvania

Fort Sill Indian School
Fort Sill, Oklahoma
Columbia Teachers College
New York, New York
**Bellevue College Medical
Hospital**
New York, New York
Harlem Hospital
(A teaching hospital)
New York, New York
Colored Waifs Home
New Orleans, Louisiana
Morgan Academy
(later Morgan State University)
Baltimore, Maryland
Barnard College
New York, New York
Columbia University
New York, New York
Wilson Junior College
Chicago, Illinois
Crane College
Chicago. Illinois
Southern Methodist University
Dallas, Texas
Dedman School of Law, SMU
Dallas, Texas
The University of Texas
Austin, Texas
Notre Dame University
Notre Dame, Indiana
The University of Illinois
Champaign, Illinois
Angelo College
(later Angelo State University),
San Angelo, Texas

Tyler Junior College
Tyler, Texas
Webster High School
Minden, Louisiana
National Chekiang University
Guizhou, China
National Southwestern
Associated University
Kunming, China
Tsung-Dao Lee Institute, Jiao
Tong University
Shanghai, China
Phillips Academy
Andover, Massachusetts
Yale University
New Haven, Connecticut
Oxford University
Oxford, England
The University of Delaware
Newark, Delaware
Syracuse University
School of Law
Syracuse, New York
Harvard University
Cambridge, Massachusetts
Harvard Law School
Cambridge, Massachusetts
North Dakota State University
Fargo, North Dakota

Stanford University
Stanford, California
Baruch College
New York, New York
Hofstra University
New York, New York
The University of New Mexico
Albuquerque, New Mexico
The University of Tennessee
Knoxville, Tennessee
The Webb School
Knoxville, Tennessee
The University of Virginia
Charlottesville, Virginia
James Madison University
Harrisonburg, Virginia
Stony Brook University
Stony Brook, New York
Xavier Institute of Management
Bhubaneswar, India
Texas Tech University
Lubbock, Texas
Lee College
Baytown, Texas
Boston University
Boston, Massachusetts
Bowdoin College
Brunswick, Maine

About the Author

John Cunyus,
author of this book,
is a retired garage painter,
shoe store clerk,
and truck driver.

Also by the Author

THE LATIN TESTAMENT PROJECT BIBLE

An English Translation of the Vulgate

Hard Cover Edition

(Searchlight Press, 2016)

THE LATIN TESTAMENT PROJECT NEW TESTAMENT

A Latin-English, Verse by Verse Translation

Hard Cover Edition

(Searchlight Press, 2013)

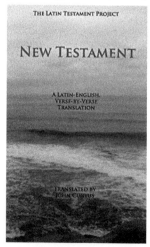

The Liberty Tree, 242

GOSPELS: MATTHEW, MARK, LUKE, JOHN
A Greek-English, Verse by Verse Translation
Soft Cover Edition
(Searchlight Press, 2017)

GRIEF RELIEF FROM THE BIBLE
A Workbook on Finding Strength
in Times of Loss
Soft Cover Edition
Searchlight Press (2017)

<u>A PATH BEYOND SUFFERING:</u>
<u>MANDALAS:</u>
<u>A Graphic Prayer Book</u>
Soft Cover Edition
Searchlight Press (2024)

Searchlight Press
Who are you looking for?
Publishers of thoughtful Christian books since 1994.
5634 Ledgestone Drive
Dallas, Texas. U. S. A.
75214-2026
www.JohnCunyus.com

The Liberty Tree, 244